Essential
English Grammar

Essential
English Grammar

By
PHILIP GUCKER

DOVER PUBLICATIONS, INC.
NEW YORK

Published in Canada by General Publishing Company, Limited, 30 Lesmill Road, Don Mills, Toronto,
Ontario.
Published in the United Kingdom by Constable
and Company, Limited.

Essential English Grammar is a new work, first
published by Dover Publications, Inc., in 1966.

International Standard Book Number: 0-486-21649-7
Library of Congress Catalog Card Number: 66-19046

Manufactured in the United States of America
Dover Publications, Inc.
180 Varick Street
New York, N.Y. 10014

TABLE OF CONTENTS

Part I

THE ESSENTIALS
OF ENGLISH GRAMMAR

In Part I you will find a clear and concise summary of English grammar: its forms, principles, and basic terminology. The material is presented in non-technical language and in easy, natural steps, beginning with the structure of the simple sentence, and continuing through the various parts of speech and other common sentence elements to the more difficult constructions. All terms and forms are amply illustrated with models and practice exercises. The section ends with "A Dictionary of Grammatical Terms," in Chapter 20, which will be useful for ready reference.

This section provides the basic principles which you will be able to apply in Part II.

THE SENTENCE:
SUBJECT AND PREDICATE

Subject and Predicate

The basic unit of written expression is the sentence.

A sentence is a group of words that says something, all by itself. It is complete; it can stand alone. It is followed by a period (or, in certain cases, a question mark or an exclamation point).

In grammatical terms, a sentence is a group of words that contains a *subject* and a *predicate*. The subject is the person or thing you're talking about. The predicate (to predicate means to say or declare) is what you're saying about it. For example:

We won.

The subject is *we*; the predicate is *won*.

Mr. Canby's house is at the end of the road.

The subject is *Mr. Canby's house*; the predicate is *is at the end of the road*.

It is fundamental that a subject or a predicate by itself doesn't say anything. It isn't a sentence. In order to form a sentence you must have *both a subject and a predicate*.

My favorite program	has been discontinued for the summer.
She	is always busy doing odd jobs around the house.
Many of the members	have resigned.
The proof of the pudding	is in the eating.

Transposed Order

You notice, of course, that in these sentences the subject comes first; that's the normal order. But you can't depend upon that. Often, for emphasis or variety, we put the predicate first (transposed order—turned around).

The winning run came across the plate. (normal order)
Across the plate came the winning run. (transposed order)

In such a sentence either way is possible; the writer has his choice.

Each example below of transposed order has been rewritten to indicate the more usual subject-predicate order:

Down the street came a ragged procession of children.
(A ragged procession of children came down the street.)
Now comes the fun.
(The fun comes now.)
On the other side of the tracks was a car dump.
(A car dump was on the other side of the tracks.)

Even more commonly the predicate may be split up, part of it coming at the beginning of the sentence, part at the end. This order is sometimes called *mixed*.

At the beginning of the season Klein was benched for weak hitting.
(Klein was benched at the beginning of the season for weak hitting.)
Suddenly I heard a voice.
(I suddenly heard a voice.)

Common sense tells you that the expressions "at the beginning of the season" and "suddenly" are not part of the person you're talking about (the subject), but part of what you're saying about him (the predicate).

Practice in Recognizing Subjects and Predicates

Draw a single line under any word that belongs with the subject, a double line under any word that belongs with the predicate.

Every word in the sentence must be underlined. Example: <u>After</u> <u>dinner</u> <u>we</u> <u>all</u> <u>sat</u> <u>around</u> <u>and</u> <u>told</u> <u>stories.</u> (Answers on page 151)

1. One of the covers is missing.
2. Mrs. Wilkinson settled down comfortably in her favorite rocker.
3. Many years ago I heard the same story with a different ending.
4. New countries in Africa and the Near East have become very important in the U.N.
5. The possibility of a voyage to the moon is no longer remote.
6. Experience is the best teacher.
7. Stamped at the head of the appeal was the single word: "Refused."
8. After many years his father returned.
9. Slowly, but with increasing speed, the water began to seep through the cracks.
10. One of the most important men in the community has gone.

KINDS OF SENTENCES

Declarative, Interrogative, Imperative, and Exclamatory Sentences*

So far, every sentence you have been working with has stated or *declared* something. Such a sentence is called *declarative*. It is followed by a period.

> That is a picture of my father.
> A car has just stopped in front of the house.

There are three other kinds of sentences.

An *interrogative* sentence asks a question:

> Is that a picture of your father?
> Has the car stopped?

Note that a question mark is used.

An *imperative* sentence commands or requests:

> Please show me the picture of your father.
> Look at the license plate.

Use a period after an imperative sentence.

An *exclamatory* sentence expresses strong and sudden emotion:

> Stop that car!
> What a picture!
> How old he looks!
> Isn't that a shame!
> How terrible!

* Classified according to the purpose for which a sentence is used. Classification according to structure will be discussed in Chapter 18.

The exclamatory sentence is different from the others: it doesn't follow any rules for sentence structure.   In fact, as you see in these examples, it may look like a question or a command.   There are only three things you can say about it:

1. It is usually short.
2. It is always dramatic or emotional.
3. It takes an exclamation point.

At this point we're going to ignore it, since the rules for subject and predicate do not apply.

Finding the Subject and Predicate

Interrogative and imperative sentences introduce some interesting problems in finding subject and predicate.

Interrogative sentences are often in transposed order.   To find the subject and predicate of such a sentence you must rephrase it as a statement (the answer expected):

Was that man at the game?
(that man was at the game)

This was partly transposed.   The subject is *that man*.

Who took my pencil?
(he took my pencil)

This was in normal order.   The subject is *who*.

Where is the best road from here to the coast?
(the best road from here to the coast is . . .)

Transposed.   The subject is *the best road from here to the coast*.

How many times must we do this?
(we must do this . . . times)

Partly transposed.   The subject is *we*.

Imperative sentences also have a slight peculiarity.   The subject is nearly always the word *you*, even though it isn't expressed.   It is called *you understood*.

(you) Please mail this letter for me.
(you) Take your time.
(you) Let me off at Canal Street.

Practice in Identifying Kinds of Sentences

Label the following sentences *D* for declarative, *Int* for interrogative, or *Imp* for imperative. Example: Please leave your wraps at the door. (*Imp*) (Answers on page 151)

1. It is very important to remember this date. (   )
2. Remember this date. (   )
3. Why did you take the book? (   )
4. He asked me about the book. (   )
5. In a situation of this kind you should take extra precautions. (   )
6. Take extra precautions. (   )
7. Please don't waste my time. (   )
8. Why has there been so much controversy about the identity of the criminal? (   )
9. Who will be the first man on the moon? (   )
10. He wants to know why. (   )

More Practice in Recognizing Subjects and Predicates

Draw a single line under any word that belongs with the subject, a double line under any word that belongs with the predicate. If the subject is *you* understood, write the word in. Example: Which of the pencils has soft lead? (Answers on page 151)

1. Take cover.
2. Only one of his many former followers remained loyal.
3. Which road will take me to the coast?
4. After Labor Day the rates are lowered considerably.
5. Where does your friend Stanley keep his car?
6. You will need a great many more tools for such a job.
7. Arrange the cards in alphabetical order.
8. Please don't bother with any of my things.
9. When does the last train for Baldwin leave today?
10. Only then did we realize the seriousness of our predicament.

3

SIMPLE SUBJECT AND VERB

Recognition of Subject and Verb

In a sentence like this:

The upper branches of the tree tossed violently in the high wind.

certain words are more essential than others. The complete subject is *The upper branches of the tree*; but the main word is *branches*. This is called the *simple subject*. The complete predicate is *tossed violently in the high wind*; but the main word is *tossed*. This is called the *verb*, or *simple predicate*.

Reduced to its essentials the sentence becomes:

branches tossed

You might call this the framework of the sentence.

Similarly, in every sentence, the main parts of the complete subject and predicate are the simple subject and the verb. From here on, when this book refers to subject and verb, the word *subject* means *simple subject*.

In order to analyze any sentence grammatically, you must be able to pick out the verb and the subject. As a rule it is easier to find the verb first, since that is the operative word, the word that makes the statement or tells what happened. Then, by asking yourself *who?* or *what?* in front of the verb, you will find the subject.

Examples:

One of our planes crash-landed safely in a ravine.
(What happened? Something *crash-landed*. That's the verb.
What *crash-landed*? The subject is *one*.)

In the doorway stood a tall gentleman with a top hat.
(Somebody *stood*—that's the verb. Who *stood*? The subject
is *gentleman*. The transposed order is no problem.)
Annabelle will be eighteen in September.
(Somebody *will be*. Who *will be*? The subject is *Annabelle*.)

The Expletive *There*

Using the same method you can work out the structure of
sentences beginning with *there*:

There is a fire in the fireplace.

The verb is *is*—a very common little verb. What *is*? The
answer is *fire*. *A fire is in the fireplace*.
Sentences of this construction are very common in English. The
word *there* is never the subject; it's a signal that the sentence is
transposed—that the subject follows the verb.

There were pictures on all the walls.
Verb: *were*. What *were*? *Pictures*.
There will be a short intermission.
Verb: *will be*. What *will be*? *Intermission*.
There is still time for one more hand.
Verb: *is*. What *is*? *Time*.

The word *there* in such a construction is called an *expletive* (something that fills out the sentence), but the name isn't important.
Just remember that *there* is not the subject.

Verb Phrases

A verb has many forms and may consist of several words—up to
four. Note the following:

Martha *broke* her doll.
Martha *is breaking* her doll.
Martha *has broken* her doll.
The doll *will break*.
The doll *has been broken*.
The doll *would have been broken*.

You can probably think of other possibilities.

A verb consisting of more than one word is called a *verb phrase*. In the sentences above, the words which have been added to *break*, or *breaking*, or *broken*, to vary the meaning or the tense, are called *auxiliaries* (helpers). They are all "verb words"; that is, they can all be used as verbs:

> She *is*.
> She *has*.
> She *will*.
> She *has been*.

And so on.

However, when a verb consists of several words, it may be interrupted by another word—or words. This is particularly true in questions:

> The doll *will* soon *be broken*.
> It *could* not *have been mended*.
> *Do* you *approve* of him?
> When *will* the work *be finished*?

You will see that these interrupting words are not "verb words" and are not therefore part of the verb.

The subject of verb forms is fairly complicated and will be studied more completely in Chapter 9, but you should now be able to recognize subjects and verbs. In the first practice exercise below, every verb is a single word; but in the second exercise remember that a verb may contain as many as four words.

Practice in Finding Subject and Verb

Underline the subject (simple subject) with a single line, the verb with a double line. Supply *you* (you understood) where necessary. Example: Against the deep blue of the sky a solitary eagle soared lazily. (Answers on page 152)

1. We cooked a five-course meal on that little stove.
2. The distance from the water supply added to our difficulty.
3. A dog of that size has a tremendous appetite.
4. Wear your overalls today.
5. I sometimes play a set or two before breakfast.
6. Please come right home after the game.

7. The little boat pitched violently on the choppy water.
8. Haven't you any copies of the latest edition?
9. There are many stories about the origin of the Christmas tree.
10. There is no need to worry.

More Practice in Finding Subject and Verb

Follow the same instructions as in the preceding exercise, but watch for verb phrases.   (Answers on page 152)

1. Two of our men were picked for the all-star game.
2. As a result of the fire two-thirds of the trees were completely destroyed.
3. I don't want any part in the affair.
4. He has often been accused unfairly.
5. Why did she decide on nursing as a career?
6. There hasn't been enough time for preparation.
7. Without your assistance many of the cattle would have been lost.
8. We cannot legitimately refuse his request.
9. Don't expect any help from me.
10. In a severe storm that weak spot in the dike would probably be pierced.

4

COMPOUND CONSTRUCTIONS

The word *compound* means *having two or more parts.* It is a word used frequently in grammar.

A subject may be compound:

> *Basketball* and *football* are challenging baseball as the national sport.
> *Boxers* and *German shepherds* are often used as Seeing-Eye dogs.
> For different temperaments, *wealth, power,* or simple *comfort* may provide the chief purpose in life.

A predicate may be compound:

> We *pushed* and *fought* our way through the crowd.
> The story *begins* well and *continues* pleasantly.
> He *tries* but seldom *succeeds.*

The words *and, or,* and *but* are called *conjunctions* (joining words). They will be discussed in Chapter 17.

When a verb phrase is compound, the auxiliaries are often omitted in the second (third, etc.) part of the compound:

> The bus *had arrived* and *departed* before dawn.
> (Actually it *had departed,* but the *had* is not repeated.)
> The book *has been praised* and *quoted* extensively.

As you study new constructions, you will see that many of them can be compound.

Practice in Finding Compound Subjects and Predicates

Underline the subject with one line, the predicate verb with two lines. If either subject or predicate is compound, write a *C* above

each part of the compound.   Example: Why don't you wait and
see the parade?   (Answers on page 152)

1. Men, women, and children were herded into the huge
   auditorium.
2. Can serious music and jazz appeal to the same person?
3. The great highways and trunk roads have increased the rate of
   automobile travel.
4. At camp we swam, sailed, or fished practically all day.
5. Gather and preserve the seeds carefully through the winter.
6. *Hamlet, Macbeth, Othello,* and *King Lear* are usually considered
   the four great tragedies of Shakespeare.
7. Most of the newspapers have criticized and condemned the
   work of the committee.
8. Strange birds and insects sang and chirped and hummed in the
   underbrush.
9. There were three cows and a new-born calf in the pasture.
10. Have you seen or heard anything about the concert?

5

COMPLEMENTS

Identification of Complements

The word *complement* (not to be confused with *compliment*) comes from the same root as the word *complete*. In grammar a complement is a word that *completes the predicate*. Its normal position is after the verb, and it is, of course, part of the predicate.

Many verbs require complements to make sense:

Harriet made ......
Jack is ......
The end of the war brought ......

The natural question is *What?* A complement can be considered anything that answers the question *What?* after a verb.

Harriet made a *cake* for the picnic.
Jack is my *cousin*.
The end of the war brought *peace* and *prosperity*.

Cake and *cousin* are complements. "*Peace* and *prosperity*" is a compound complement.

A complement, unlike the subject and the verb, is not an essential part of every sentence. Some verbs do not require complements:

The ship disappeared over the horizon.
He talks incessantly.
Finally the train stopped.

Disappeared what? Talks what? Stopped what? The question doesn't come up; hence there is no complement.

Transitive and Intransitive

Your dictionary will tell you that the verb *bring* is a *v.t.*, while *disappear* is a *v.i.* Those abbreviations are related to this matter of complements. *V.t.* means *verb transitive*; *v.i.* means *verb intransitive.* Both words contain the Latin root *trans*, meaning "across." When we use a transitive verb, the action is carried across the verb to a complement. When we use an intransitive verb, the action terminates with the verb.

Some verbs may be either. "Stop," for example, is a *v.t.* (The engineer stopped the train.) or a *v.i.* (The train stopped.).

In Chapter 8 the discussion of different kinds of verbs includes further information on complements. For the present the question *What?* will serve to identify the complement of any verb. But naturally, in order to find the complement you must first find the verb.

Practice in Finding Complements

Identify the complement in each sentence by writing a *C* above it. If there is no complement write *NC* after the sentence. Example: You should call the office for advice. (Answers on page 153)

1. The paprika is a very important ingredient in this dish.
2. The lion roared a challenge at the intruders.
3. Divide the work evenly.
4. You should certainly finish before three o'clock.
5. Why did you bring all these bags and boxes with you?
6. The picture will be shown again at ten o'clock.
7. She has been practicing medicine for a number of years.
8. The new student and her mother were waiting in the reception room.
9. In many communities natural gas has replaced the artificial product.
10. Have another slice.

Practice in Finding Subjects, Verbs, and Complements

Identify the subject (one line), the verb (two lines), and the complement (*C*). If there is no complement write *NC*. Example:

C
Everybody wants a leading part in the play.　(Answers on page 153)

1. George has been reading steadily for several days.
2. George has been reading the same book for several days.
3. Don't bother me with your troubles.
4. The *Queen Mary* was sailing slowly up the harbor.
5. Have you noticed any change in his manner?
6. There is no time for idle dreaming.
7. You must give time and attention to this problem.
8. The city stretches along the lake shore for miles.
9. Why is Mr. Henry carrying the flag?
10. Take your hat and coat and leave the house.

6

PREPOSITIONAL PHRASES

Phrases; Prepositions and Their Objects

A *phrase* may be any short group of words. It's a convenient term in grammar. A *prepositional phrase* is simply a particular kind of phrase; but it is so common in English—and so easy to identify—that you might as well get used to it from the start. If you can recognize the prepositional phrases in a sentence, you will be able to sort out the rest of the sentence more easily.

A prepositional phrase looks like this:

to the store	at school	under the table
with me	for a week	on time
between meals	of my brother	after dinner
in the office	near the road	off the roof

A *preposition* (literally, a word that *is placed before* another word) is the first word in the phrase: *to, at, under, with*, etc. It is followed by a word standing for a person or thing, called the *object* of the preposition. *Store, school, table, me*, etc., are the objects of the prepositions. The preposition shows a relationship. A thing may be *under* the table, *at* the table, *on* the table, *by* the table, *between* the table and the wall (compound object).

A longer list of prepositions will be found in Chapter 16.

There may be other words in the phrase, coming between the preposition and its object:

after dinner
after a good dinner
after a very hasty dinner

In any case, the phrase begins with a preposition and ends with the object of the preposition.

A knowledge of prepositional phrases will help you to avoid confusion in identifying subjects and complements. Thus:

> Two (of the boys) were caught. (The subject is *two*.)
> We examined a large assortment (of rings). (The complement is *assortment*.)
> The committee (on membership) faces one (of the most unpleasant tasks) (in its history). (The subject is *committee*; the complement is *one*.)

Infinitives

WARNING: *To* is a common preposition; but when *to* is followed by a form of a verb, instead of a noun or pronoun, the construction is called an *infinitive*, and is not to be confused with a prepositional phrase.

These are prepositional phrases:

> to her, to school, to the meeting, to the end

These are infinitives:

> to go, to read, to understand, to bargain

Infinitives will be discussed in Chapter 10.

Practice in Recognizing Prepositional Phrases

In the sentences below draw parentheses around every prepositional phrase. Example: The struggle (between the leaders) (of the two groups) involved many (of the other members). (Answers on page 154)

1. The trend of women's fashions changes rapidly from year to year.
2. The children eat a good deal of candy between meals.
3. He plays a game of chess every night after dinner.
4. On the workbench were a plane and a beautiful new set of chisels.
5. He lives in a house by the side of the road.

6. The injured man was transferred from the trawler to a coast-guard vessel.
7. Tie the end of the line around a pole.
8. By the end of the day we were exhausted.
9. Many of the men on the project refused to work overtime. (BE CAREFUL WITH THIS ONE.)
10. Visitors must enter through this door and leave by the door at the other side.

7

PARTS OF SPEECH

The phrase *parts of speech* means simply "the different jobs that words do in sentences." Since there are seven such jobs to be done, there are seven essential parts of speech—plus an eighth which has no regular job.

1. *verb:* a word that expresses an action or makes a statement.
2. *noun:* a specific word for a person, a place, a thing, a quality, etc.
3. *pronoun:* a stand-in for a noun.
4. *adjective:* a word that modifies a noun or a pronoun. (To modify is to limit or point out or describe: *that* book; *another* chance; *the blue* ribbon). For convenience the articles *a, an,* and *the* are usually classified under adjectives.
5. *adverb:* a word that modifies a verb, an adjective, or another adverb.
6. *preposition:* a word that connects a noun or a pronoun to some other word in a sentence—to make a prepositional phrase.
7. *conjunction:* a word that connects various words and groups of words.

The bracketing shows you how these parts of speech are related in their functions.

Finally, to be complete, we must list one other:

8. *interjection:* an exclamatory word (ouch! hey! alas!), which has no grammatical relationship to the rest of the sentence. It need not bother us here.

In the following chapters the seven essential parts of speech will be examined in detail. However, you can get the feeling by seeing them at work in the sentences below:

NOUN   VERB
Harry was studying.

VERB ADJ ADJ NOUN PREP PRO
Give the other book to   me.

PRO   VERB ADJ NOUN CON NOUN
Somebody forgot the salt and pepper.

NOUN CON   NOUN   VERB   ADJ ADJ NOUN
Skiing and snowshoeing require strong leg muscles.

ADJ   ADJ   NOUN VERB ADJ ADV   ADJ   NOUN
The French poodle is   a   very intelligent dog.

PRO PREP ADJ   NOUN   PREP NOUN   VERB   PREP
Many of the properties of radium were discovered by
        NOUN
Madame Curie.

CON ADJ NOUN VERB ADV ADJ PRO VERB   ADV
Since the weather was not cold, we stayed outdoors.

The part of speech of a word depends upon its use in a particular sentence. Note the following:

Put on the *light*. (noun)
Light the gas. (verb)
Howard is too *light* for football. (adj)
Can you lend me a *pencil*? (noun)
He keeps a *pencil* tray on his desk. (adj)
One *leg* seems shorter than the other. (noun)
He tore a *leg* muscle. (adj)
I *long* for peace and quiet. (verb)
It was a *long* trip. (adj)
Don't work too *long*. (adv)
That book belongs to me. (adj)
That is my book. (pro)
His work is finished. (adj)
This hammer must be *his*. (pro)

The *well* has gone dry.   (noun)
He writes *well*.   (adv)
He is *well*.   (adj)
The meeting was put *off*.   (adv)
It was blown *off* the roof.   (prep)

One further significant fact: In subsequent chapters, when we discuss various word groups, you will find that they are used as one or another of these seven parts of speech. The prepositional phrases in Chapter 6, for example, are always used as modifiers— like adjectives or adverbs.

Practice in Using Parts of Speech

For each of the words listed below, write several sentences, using the word as each of the various parts of speech indicated.   (Answers on page 154)

1. *love*—verb, noun, adjective
2. *back*—verb, noun, adverb
3. *right*—adjective, adverb
4. *fast*—verb, noun, adjective, adverb
5. *any*—pronoun, adjective

Practice in Recognizing Parts of Speech

Using abbreviations like those used in the illustrative sentences above, tell what part of speech each word is by writing the abbreviation above the word.   (Answers on page 154)

1. We must get across the Swiss border by midnight.
2. Will Carmen pay for the broken window?
3. Every one of the students has received a letter from the principal or his secretary.
4. The bindings of many books have been hopelessly ruined.
5. This car can be repaired, but the other is a wreck.

8

VERBS: TWO KINDS; AND
COMPLEMENTS

Linking and Action Verbs

The verb is the heart of the predicate and usually the most important part of the sentence.

In any language the topic of verbs is large, and rather complicated. This chapter deals with the two major kinds of English verbs, and how to recognize them.

No one has ever invented a foolproof definition for a verb, but the simplest definition is probably the most useful: *A verb is a word that expresses* (1) *action or* (2) *state of being.* Hence the two main kinds of verbs are *action verbs* (*go, see, want, talk, behave, need,* etc.) and *state of being* or *linking* verbs (*is, was, has been,* etc.; and *seem, smell, look, remain,* etc.).

By this classification, action verbs include not only such obvious words as *run, fight, sneeze,* but words like *rest, die, hope.* These are all called action verbs for want of a better term. If this classification seems confusing, we might state the difference like this:

An action verb tells what something *is, was, will be doing*:

> The old lady *died* last night.
> Mother *needs* your help.
> I *don't recognize* the name.

The subjects are doing something.

A linking verb tells what something *is, was, will be*:

> Otto *will be* our next captain.
> The salad *tastes* bad.
> The weather *remains* unsettled.

The subjects aren't doing anything.

Certain verbs—*smell, taste, look*, etc.—can be either linking verbs or action verbs, depending on their use:

He *looked* tired. (not doing anything)
He *looked* intently at the picture. (doing something)
He *tasted* the sauce. (doing something)
It *tasted* too bitter. (not doing anything)

The most common linking verb is the verb *be*—a very irregular verb. These are some of its forms: *am, are, is, was, were, has been, have been, had been, will be, will have been.*

He *is* a soldier.
He *was* a soldier.
He *has been* a soldier.

Two Kinds of Complements

There is another significant difference between the two kinds of verbs. They show a different relationship to the *complement* (see Chapter 5).

With an *action verb*, the subject acts upon the complement:

Mother *needs* help.
Jack *took* his book with him.
I *don't recognize* the name.

Help, book, and *name* are called *direct objects* of the verbs.

With a *linking verb*, the subject is linked to the complement—identified with or described by the complement:

Otto *will be* the next captain. (*Otto* and *captain* are the same person.)
That *was* a very interesting picture. (*That* and *picture* are the same thing.)
The weather *remains* unsettled. (*unsettled* describes *weather*.)

Picture, captain, and *unsettled* are called *predicate complements.* Predicate complements, if they stand for the subject, like *captain* and *picture*, are called *predicate nominatives.* They are nouns (or possibly pronouns). If they describe the subject, like *unsettled*, they are called *predicate adjectives*.

> He is a good *man*. (predicate nominative—*man* and *he* are the same)
> He is very *good* at his work. (predicate adjective—*good* describes *he*)
> Her story was a complete *lie*. (predicate nominative—*lie* and *story* are the same)
> Her story was *false*. (predicate adjective—*false* describes *story*)

Reminder: Forms of the verb *be* are often used as auxiliary verbs (see Chapter 3). In such cases, of course, the entire verb phrase must be considered. *Was* by itself is a linking verb; *was going* is an action verb.

Indirect Objects

In addition to direct objects and predicate complements, there is a construction called the *indirect object*, sometimes used after action verbs. It occurs usually in sentences which already contain a direct object.

> He gave *me* a dollar.
> He told his *mother* a story.
> She baked *us* a cake.

One test of an indirect object is that it can be expressed alternately by a prepositional phrase introduced by *to* or *for*:

> He gave a dollar *to me*.
> He told a story *to his mother*.
> She baked a cake *for us*.

Hence an indirect object is a noun or pronoun which precedes a direct object (expressed or implied) and answers the question: *to or for whom?*

Illustrated below are some of the various possible combinations, with different kinds of verbs and complements:

> Everybody waited quietly. (action verb, no complement)
> There should be a new picture next week. (linking verb, no

complement, since *there* is an expletive, and *picture* is the
subject)

Mrs. Lenz searched the room carefully.   (action verb, direct
object)

Mother wrote us a long letter.   (action verb, indirect object,
direct object)

I have never been a serious student.   (linking verb, predicate
nominative)

The responsibility is mine.   (linking verb, predicate nominative)

The view from the summit is magnificent.   (linking verb,
predicate adjective)

Practice in Recognizing Complements

Label all complements in the sentences below, as follows: direct
object (*DO*), predicate nominative (*PN*), predicate adjective (*PA*),
indirect object (*IO*). If there is no complement, write *NC*.
(Answers on page 155)

1. The summer continued hot and dry.
2. This condition increased the danger of forest fires.
3. Don't tell anyone the truth about my new job.
4. There was just one man in the room.
5. You shouldn't send her such a curt note.
6. One of the apples is wormy.
7. After all that hullaballoo, nothing happened.
8. I want twenty of these and ten of those.
9. Saul will be a lieutenant by the end of the year.
10. You must pay the man his fee.

FORMS AND PROPERTIES OF VERBS

Principal Parts; Irregular Verbs

In one way English verbs are comparatively easy: they do not change their form very much. A so-called *regular* verb, like *talk*, or *offer*, or *decline*, has only four possible forms:

talk	talks	talked	talking
offer	offers	offered	offering
decline	declines	declined	declining

Even the irregular verbs have at most five possible forms:

do	does	did	doing	done
give	gives	gave	giving	given
see	sees	saw	seeing	seen

(The verb *be*, described in Chapter 8, is unique; it has many irregular forms.)

The many meanings which a verb may express are obtained by adding a variety of auxiliary verbs to these basic forms.

The fundamental forms of the verb are called the *principal parts*; and the proper use of an irregular verb depends on a knowledge of these principal parts: *present* (with a slight change for third person singular), *past*, *present participle*, and *past participle*. The regular verbs offer no problem, since the past and past participle are identical in form, with a *-d* or *-ed* added to the present.

These are some of the irregular verbs you should master. Use this list for reference.

PRESENT	PAST	PRESENT PARTICIPLE	PAST PARTICIPLE
bear/bears	bore	bearing	(have) borne
beat/beats	beat	beating	(have) beaten
begin/begins	began	beginning	(have) begun
bite/bites	bit	biting	(have) bitten
blow/blows	blew	blowing	(have) blown
break/breaks	broke	breaking	(have) broken
bring/brings	brought	bringing	(have) brought
burst/bursts	burst	bursting	(have) burst
catch/catches	caught	catching	(have) caught
choose/chooses	chose	choosing	(have) chosen
come/comes	came	coming	(have) come
creep/creeps	crept	creeping	(have) crept
cut/cuts	cut	cutting	(have) cut
*dive/dives	dived	diving	(have) dived
do/does	did	doing	(have) done
draw/draws	drew	drawing	(have) drawn
drink/drinks	drank	drinking	(have) drunk
drive/drives	drove	driving	(have) driven
eat/eats	ate	eating	(have) eaten
fall/falls	fell	falling	(have) fallen
flee/flees	fled	fleeing	(have) fled
fling/flings	flung	flinging	(have) flung
fly/flies	flew	flying	(have) flown
forget/forgets	forgot	forgetting	(have) forgotten
freeze/freezes	froze	freezing	(have) frozen
get/gets	got	getting	(have) got, gotten
give/gives	gave	giving	(have) given
go/goes	went	going	(have) gone
grow/grows	grew	growing	(have) grown
hang/hangs (execute)	hanged	hanging	(have) hanged
hang/hangs (suspend)	hung	hanging	(have) hung
hurt/hurts	hurt	hurting	(have) hurt
know/knows	knew	knowing	(have) known

* This, as you see, is a regular verb; but in colloquial use the past is *dove*.

PRESENT	PAST	PRESENT PARTICIPLE	PAST PARTICIPLE
lay/lays (put)	laid	laying	(have) laid
lead/leads	led	leading	(have) led
lend/lends	lent	lending	(have) lent
lie/lies (recline)	lay	lying	(have) lain
lie/lies (tell a lie)	lied	lying	(have) lied
lose/loses	lost	losing	(have) lost
ride/rides	rode	riding	(have) ridden
ring/rings	rang	ringing	(have) rung
rise/rises	rose	rising	(have) risen
run/runs	ran	running	(have) run
say/says	said	saying	(have) said
see/sees	saw	seeing	(have) seen
set/sets	set	setting	(have) set
shake/shakes	shook	shaking	(have) shaken
*shine/shines	shone	shining	(have) shone
sing/sings	sang	singing	(have) sung
sink/sinks	sank	sinking	(have) sunk
sit/sits	sat	sitting	(have) sat
slay/slays	slew	slaying	(have) slain
speak/speaks	spoke	speaking	(have) spoken
spring/springs	sprang	springing	(have) sprung
steal/steals	stole	stealing	(have) stolen
sting/stings	stung	stinging	(have) stung
swear/swears	swore	swearing	(have) sworn
swim/swims	swam	swimming	(have) swum
swing/swings	swung	swinging	(have) swung
take/takes	took	taking	(have) taken
tear/tears	tore	tearing	(have) torn
throw/throws	threw	throwing	(have) thrown
wear/wears	wore	wearing	(have) worn
weep/weeps	wept	weeping	(have) wept
write/writes	wrote	writing	(have) written

* These are the forms for the intransitive verb (The sun *shone* brightly). But the transitive verb (He *shined* shoes) has a regular past and past participle.

Auxiliary Verbs

The *auxiliary verbs*—those words which may be added to the principal parts to form *verb phrases* (see page 10)—belong to a specific and limited group. The verb forms listed below are those which can be used to begin a verb phrase:

do	can	am	have
does	could	are	has
did	shall	is	had
may	should	was	
might	will	were	
must	would		

The verbs in the *first two columns* combine only with the naming form of the verb: e.g., *go, break, freeze, see, take*:

She *did*n't *go* to the party.
It *may break* any minute.
You *will freeze* without a coat.
We *could see* the distant mountains.
I *can take* another passenger.

In the passive voice the auxiliaries in this group combine with the naming form of the verb *be*, followed by a past participle: e.g., *may be broken, will be frozen, could be seen*.

The verbs in the *third column* can combine with the present participle: e.g., *choosing, singing, speaking*:

He *is choosing* his words carefully.
The tenors *are singing* off key.
We *were speaking* together recently.

The verbs in the *third and fourth columns* can combine with the past participle: e.g., *broken, forgotten, slain, written*:

The dam *is broken*.
All their good intentions *were forgotten*.
He *has slain* his friend.
We *had received* several letters from her.

The words in the last two columns—the forms of the verbs *be* and *have*—are the most common auxiliaries. Verb phrases of three or four words are formed by using combinations of these between the first auxiliary and the main verb form: *must be taken, will have been chosen, is being written, might have seen, will be working, should have been going.*

Properties of Verbs

In actual use in a sentence, any verb has five properties: *person, number, tense, voice,* and *mood.*

Person and *number* affect the verb form only in the present tense. The *s* ending listed in the principal parts (*plays, goes*) is the form of the present tense, third person, singular number.   Thus:

	SINGULAR	PLURAL
1ST PERSON	I *play*, or *go*	we *play*, or *go*
2ND PERSON	you *play*, or *go*	you *play*, or *go*
3RD PERSON	he *plays*, or *goes*	they *play*, or *go*

The verb *be* is the only one that is more radically affected by person and number.   Changes occur not only in the present but also in the past:

	PRESENT		PAST	
	SINGULAR	PLURAL	SINGULAR	PLURAL
1ST PERSON	I *am*	we *are*	I *was*	we *were*
2ND PERSON	you *are*	you *are*	you *were*	you *were*
3RD PERSON	he *is*	they *are*	he *was*	they *were*

Note: The section on personal pronouns in Chapter 12 includes a more extensive discussion of *person.*

Tense

Tense is the method of indicating time.   There are six standard tenses:

Present: I *go*	Present Perfect: I *have gone*
Past: I *went*	Past Perfect: I *had gone*
Future: I *will* (*shall*) *go*	Future Perfect: I *will* (*shall*) *have gone*

In addition there are so-called *progressive* forms for the same six tenses, made up of the auxiliary verb *be* plus the present participle (*-ing* ending):

Present: I *am going*   Present Perfect: I *have been going*
Past: I *was going*   Past Perfect: I *had been going*
Future: I *will (shall) be*   Future Perfect: I *will (shall) have*
          going   *been going*

Each of the six tenses has particular uses, not always clearly indicated by the name of the tense. The explanations should be studied carefully.

Present Tense

The *present tense* regularly expresses something occurring now, in the present: He *works* here. We *need* help.

Where continuing action is emphasized, the *present progressive* is used: The system *is working* very well. She *is sleeping* quietly now.

The present tense is also used for:

Habitual action: He always *needs* more help than the others. She *takes* a walk every morning.

Past time in narrative (historical present), for dramatic effect: In the village they *hear* the rapid beat of hoofs. A riderless horse *dashes* in and *stands* with heaving flanks.

Future time: We *leave* for home tomorrow. He *takes* German next term.

Past Tense

The *past tense* is used to express something that occurred in the past but did not continue into the present: He *worked* here last summer. She *fell* from the ladder and *broke* her wrist.

The *past progressive*, like the present progressive, expresses continuing action—action moving through a specific period in the past: I knew she *was falling*, but I could not catch her. The system *was working* very well until you came.

Compare the use of the past tense with the present perfect and past perfect below.

Future Tense

The *future* and *future progressive tenses*, formed with *will* or *shall*, are used to express action in the future: Time *will tell*. *Will* you *come* by ship? I *will be waiting* for you. Everybody *will be leaving* soon.

See also the use of present tense to express future time.

Note on *will* and *shall*: The traditional distinctions between *shall* and *will* are not consistently observed even by careful speakers and writers.

The older theory is that *shall* is used in the first person, *will* in the second or third person, to express the simple future (expectation or probability):

> We *shall* probably find them on the beach.
> You *will* see many changes since your last visit.
> He *will* want his dinner.

Reversing this arrangement, *will* is used in the first person, *shall* in the second or third person, to express will or determination on the part of the speaker:

> I *will* do my best.
> You *shall* go when I tell you to go.
> He *shall* have me to answer to.

In practice the use of *shall*, as illustrated above, is not necessary, and probably not usual.   *Will* or *'ll* can safely be substituted:

> We'*ll* probably find them on the beach.
> You *will* go when I tell you to go.
> He *will* have me to answer to.

The use of *shall* to express determination in the second or third person is still sometimes preferred for its literary or rhetorical flavor. It is also common in legal language:

> Thou *shalt* not kill.
> They *shall* not pass.
> You *shall* die.
> Persons guilty of such offenses *shall* be required . . .

For ordinary speaking and writing, however, there is only one use of *shall* which can really be considered essential: In polite questions in the first person, where the person addressed is being given a choice:

> *Shall* we dance?
> *Shall* I invite Bertha?
> *Shall* I write in ink?
> *Shall* we take the car?

Aside from this, and except in very formal situations, it is safest and simplest to use *will* or *'ll* for all purposes.

PRESENT PERFECT TENSE

The present perfect tense is another way of referring to an action in the past (see past tense); but whereas past tense refers to a time in the past cut off from the present, the present perfect refers generally to a period of time carried up to the present:

Past: He *finished* last night.
Present Perfect: He *has* just *finished*.
Past: I *worked* there for three summers.   (in the past)
Present Perfect: I'*ve worked* there every summer.   (still doing it)

The *present perfect progressive* emphasizes that the action, begun in the past, is still going on:

I *have been taking* vitamin pills.
She *has been sleeping* for several hours.

PAST PERFECT TENSE

The *past perfect tense* is used to indicate that a past occurrence was earlier in time than some other past occurrence:

When I *had read* half the book, I discovered that the last chapter was missing.   (First I *had read*; then I *discovered*)
We realized that we *had forgotten* our tickets.
We realized that we *had been living* too expensively.

FUTURE PERFECT TENSE

The *future perfect tense* is used to indicate that an occurrence in the future is earlier than some other occurrence in the future:

By the time we get there, Harry *will have gone*.
When I finish this term, I *will have been* here for three years.

The progressive is rarely used in the future perfect.

Voice and Mood

The choice of *active* or *passive voice* is not a grammatical problem. For effective expression your choice will depend on the point of view you want to emphasize:

Active voice: The audience *applauded* her performance.
               Our men *are hitting* the ball well.

Passive voice: Her performance *was applauded* by the audience.
Their pitcher *is being hit* hard.

Mood is also of little practical importance here, except insofar as the *subjunctive mood* continues to play a part in certain expressions.

The changing language has resulted in the gradual abandonment of the subjunctive mood except for one very limited purpose: when expressing a condition contrary to fact, in an *if* clause, or after a verb which expresses a wish. Specifically, we use the word *were* instead of *was* in such expressions:

> If I *were* you, I'd quit right now.
> She acts as if she *were* my mother.
> I wish I *were* there.
> If she *were* at home, she would answer the bell.

It is clear in the *if* sentences (conditions) that I am not you, that she is not my mother, etc.; hence the term "contrary to fact."

Summary

Every verb in actual use has five properties: *person, number, tense, voice,* and *mood.* In even the simplest sentence:

> I *saw* you at the beach.

the verb *saw* is first person, singular number, past tense, active voice, indicative mood. Again, in:

> He *wants* to go out.

the verb *wants* is third person, singular number, present tense, active voice, indicative mood.

Most of this information, while useful for an understanding of grammatical constructions, has no functional application. For practical purposes the main points to remember are these:

Number: If a verb is in present tense, third person, the verb must be singular if the subject is singular, plural if the subject is plural.

Tense: Particularly in the various ways of indicating past tense, care must be used.

Mood: Certain constructions require the subjunctive mood.

Practice in Using Verb Forms

Fill in the correct form of the irregular verb named at the beginning of each sentence, and tell whether it is the past (*P*) or the past participle (*PP*). Example: *bring* Sam <u>brought</u> his little brother because his mother insisted. (*P*)   (Answers on page 155)

1. *freeze*   Most of us were nearly _____. (   )

2. *fly*   He could have _____ to Chicago in that time. (   )

3. *drink*   Who _____ the glass of milk I left here? (   )

4. *begin*   We could have _____ much earlier. (   )

5. *take*   Why couldn't he have _____ me with him? (   )

6. *run*   Suddenly the car swerved and _____ right into the fence. (   )

7. *swim*   I think you _____ very well in yesterday's race. (   )

8. *fall*   She couldn't have _____ more than ten feet. (   )

9. *ride*   Dad thought we had _____ far enough for one day. (   )

10. *see*   Kermit _____ the whole show twice. (   )

11. *throw*   Riley swung around and _____ the ball to third. (   )

12. *steal*   Someone had _____ my sneakers. (   )

13. *drive*   Have you ever _____ over the Cabot Trail? (   )

14. *choose*   At the last meeting we _____ a new captain. (   )

15. *know*   I _____ most of the answers, but I couldn't concentrate. (   )

16. *burst*   At first we thought the water pipes had _____. (   )

17. *go*   The bus had _____ when we got there. (   )

18. *do*   Maria says she _____ what she could.
             (   )
19. *speak* After the riot the principal _____ to
             several students.   (   )
20. *write* You should have _____ in ink.   (   )

Practice in Identifying the Perfect Tenses

Underline the verbs in perfect tenses (complete verb phrases), and tell whether they are present perfect (*Pr*), past perfect (*P*), or future perfect (*F*). Be watchful for the progressive as well as the simple tense forms. Example: Things <u>had been going</u> from bad to worse. (*P*) (Answers on page 155)

1. I'm sure they have arrived by now.   (   )
2. It seems to me you have been complaining a great deal.
   (   )
3. So far I have not been speaking of political differences.   (   )
4. The constitution has changed with the times.   (   )
5. We have learned something from Freud about the terrors of childhood.   (   )
6. At least I will have satisfied myself about his honesty.   (   )
7. He had barely reached the summit when the blizzard began.
   (   )
8. Mrs. Morgan has not hitherto shown any interest in my work.
   (   )
9. We had been plodding along steadily all day.   (   )
10. If they take this one, they will have won six straight.   (   )

VERBALS

The difference between a verbal and a verb is basically in the way it is used in a sentence. A verbal can be used as a noun, an adjective, or an adverb; it is never a verb. However, it is derived from a verb, and it looks something like a verb.

There are three kinds of verbals: *infinitives*, *participles*, and *gerunds*.

Infinitives

An *infinitive* is generally a form of a verb preceded by *to*. It looks like this: *to go, to swim, to laugh, to have written, to be considered.* It may be present or perfect, active or passive:

	ACTIVE	PASSIVE
PRESENT:	to see, to steal	to be seen, to be stolen
PERFECT:	to have seen	to have been seen
	to have stolen	to have been stolen

After certain verbs the so-called "sign of the infinitive" *to* is often omitted. The following sentences contain infinitives without *to*:

Help him *move* that sofa.
Watch the fish *snap* at the hook.
Can you feel the floor *move*?
Let us *resolve* that this shall never happen again.

Verbs which can be followed by this construction are *see, hear, feel, help, let, make, watch.*

The infinitive has three possible functions:

As a noun:
I hate *to go*. (noun object)
To have fallen would have been fatal. (noun subject)

39

As an adjective:
It's time *to go*.   (modifies *time*)
There are plenty of jobs *to be done*.   (modifies *jobs*)

As an adverb:
He always plays *to win*.   (modifies the verb *plays*)
We were unable *to go*.   (modifies the adjective *unable*)
To be fully *informed*, read your local newspaper.   (modifies the verb *read*)

Like all verbals, an infinitive may have adverbial modifiers, and it may take any form of complement that a verb takes.   The group of words so formed is called an *infinitive phrase*:

We expect *to leave the house early*.   (object, plus adverbial modifier)
I want *to be happy*.   (predicate adjective)
It was foolish *to lend him the money*.   (indirect object plus direct object)

The difference between the present and perfect infinitives must be carefully observed in practice.   The present infinitive, which is far the most common, is used to indicate the same time as the main verb, or later:

He tries *to go* faster.
He tried *to go* faster.
He will try *to go* faster.

The perfect infinitive is used only to indicate time earlier than that of the main verb:

He would like *to have gone* faster.
I'm glad *to have had* this talk with you.
(Compare: I'm glad *to be having* this talk with you.)
He is reported *to have eaten* nothing for three days.
(Compare: He expects *to eat* nothing for three days.)

The term "split infinitive" refers to a construction in which a word, usually an adverb, intervenes between *to* and the verb form: "to always cooperate," "to thoroughly understand."   It is usually awkward and generally disapproved of.   Avoid it if possible by rephrasing:

It is our aim always *to cooperate* . . .
To understand this question thoroughly . . .

Participles

Two of the principal parts of a verb are the present and past participles: *going, gone*; *stating, stated*. They are commonly used with auxiliary verbs to form verb phrases: *is going, was stated, has been stated*. When these forms are used without auxiliaries, they are verbals. Used as adjectives, to modify nouns or pronouns, they are called simply *participles*.

A simple participle is used exactly like an adjective, next to its noun: a *startling* statement; the *strolling* players; the *abandoned* house.

A participial phrase may appear in any of several positions in a sentence, but it usually modifies the subject of the sentence:

Laughing gaily, she turned away.   (modifies *she*)

Shaking his fist at me, he walked back to the car.   (modifies *he*)

Seen from across the valley, the red roofs are very distinct.   (modifies *roofs*)

The auctioneer, *pausing for a moment*, looked down into the crowd.   (modifies *auctioneer*)

The candles *lighted in the living room* looked very gay.   (modifies *candles*)

He showed us the book *opened at the first page*.   (modifies the object, *book*)

Gerunds

A *gerund* looks like a present participle; it always ends in *-ing*: *going, writing, swimming, adventuring*.

It is always used as a noun.   Some grammar books call it a noun participle.

His *skating* is remarkable.   (subject)

She enjoys *lying in the hammock*.   (object)

Playing a musical instrument affords relaxation.   (subject)

Mr. Jones objects to your *using his lawn*.   (object of preposition)

Practice in Recognizing Infinitives

Underline all infinitive phrases in the following sentences. Watch out for infinitives without *to*.   Label each one noun (N),

N
adjective *(Adj)*, or adverb *(Adv)*.   Example: Try <u>to see it my way.</u>
(Answers on page 156)

1. One way to achieve success is to see your goal clearly.
2. He is afraid to say anything.
3. I'm proud to have been one of your assistants.
4. Will you help me move this sofa?
5. His worst mistake was to reject his father's help.
6. I'd like to hear from the other members.
7. Watch the dust fly when Simpson starts.
8. I need a screwdriver to loosen this.
9. It's almost time to go.
10. To tell you the truth, I'll be glad to quit.

Practice in Recognizing Participles and Gerunds

Underline all participial and gerund phrases in the following sentences, and label them participle *(P)* or gerund *(G)*.   Example:
P
<u>Seeing the multitude</u>, he went up into a mountain.   (Answers on page 156)

1. Trespassing is forbidden.
2. Dryberg was arrested for breaking into his own house.
3. A little woman, trembling with fright, ran up the steps.
4. Abandoned by everyone, the child was weeping bitterly.
5. Training dogs is a highly skilled profession.
6. Watching his chance, he suddenly leaped for the window.
7. Having given formal notice, I made preparations for leaving.
8. Mother has no objection to your going.
9. A dead tree trunk, covered with ivy, stood in the yard.
10. Engrossed in his book, he did not notice the intruders.

NOUNS

Recognition of Nouns

A *noun* is a "name."

Any word that stands for something you're talking about—a subject, an object, or a predicate nominative, for example—is either a noun or a pronoun. The difference is essentially that a noun has a meaning by itself: *boy, college, life, evil*; whereas a pronoun, like *he, that, somebody*, acquires meaning only upon being used in some particular situation.

Another distinction is that nouns can be modified by articles and adjectives: *my boy, the junior college, an easy life.* Pronouns generally do not take such modifiers.

The term *noun* includes not only a person, place, or concrete thing, but also a quality (*blackness, fear, humility*), an action (*writing, resistance, treatment*), or an abstract concept (*belief, majority, art*). Words in these last three classes are called *abstract nouns*.

Our concern with nouns, aside from the question of recognition, is mainly to deal with three problems in writing:

How to capitalize correctly.
How to form plurals correctly.
How to form possessives correctly.

Proper Nouns

The name of a particular person, place, or thing is called a *proper noun.* The first letter of such a word is capitalized.

Capitalize people's names, names of political and geographical places, names of particular buildings or streets or events, languages, nationalities, or religions. The list of illustrations will help you to distinguish between the particular and the general:

North America	a large continent
Hyde Park High School	in high school
Wagner College	a college graduate
St. Luke's Hospital	in the hospital
the Middle West	traveling west
the Far East	east of the river
Irishman	journalist
American Indians	natives
The President addressed Congress	the president of my club
Roman Catholic	becoming a priest

Capitalize references to the Deity and the Bible: *God, Old Testament*; but *the Greek gods, sacred books of the Hindus.*

Capitalize names of planets or constellations, but not the sun, the moon, or the earth: *Mars, Saturn, the Big Dipper, stars, planets.*

Capitalize days of the week and names of months, but not names of seasons: *Wednesday, December, summer, winter.*

Plurals

Most nouns add *s* to form the plural: *tool, tools*; *rake, rakes*; *subject, subjects*; *quilt, quilts.*

Nouns ending in *s, x, z, sh,* and *ch,* add *es* to form the plural; otherwise they would be unpronounceable: *loss, losses*; *tax, taxes*; *church, churches.*

Some nouns ending in *o* preceded by a consonant, add *es* to form the plural: *echo, echoes*; *hero, heroes*; *Negro, Negroes*; *potato, potatoes*; *torpedo, torpedoes.* But some such nouns, particularly musical terms from the Italian, take only *s*: *piano, pianos*; *soprano, sopranos*; *cello, cellos*; and words ending in *o* preceded by a vowel take *s*: *cameo, cameos*; *folio, folios*; *radio, radios.*

Some nouns ending in *f* or *fe* change the *f* to *v* and add *es* (or *s* if there is already an *e*) to form the plural: *calf, calves*; *half, halves*; *knife, knives*; *thief, thieves*; *wife, wives.*

But other nouns ending in *f* or *fe* are regular: *belief, beliefs*; *handkerchief, handkerchiefs*; *roof, roofs*; *safe, safes.*

Nouns ending in *y* preceded by a consonant change the *y* to *i* and add *es* to form the plural: *army, armies; fly, flies; lady, ladies; rally, rallies.*

But nouns ending in *y* preceded by a vowel are regular: *toy, toys; donkey, donkeys; valley, valleys.*

In addition to these larger groups, all of which add either *s* or *es* for the plural, there are a number of small groups of nouns with special plurals:

> no change: *sheep, sheep; deer, deer; fish, fish; species, species*
> internal changes: *foot, feet; tooth, teeth; mouse, mice; man, men*
> adding *en*: *ox, oxen; child, children*
> *a* to *ae*: *alumna* (feminine), *alumnae; nebula, nebulae; vertebra, vertebrae*
> *us* to *i*: *alumnus* (masculine), *alumni; radius, radii; stimulus, stimuli*
> *um* to *a*: *memorandum, memoranda; medium, media; datum, data*
> *is* to *es*: *basis, bases; oasis, oases; thesis, theses*
> *on* to *a*: *criterion, criteria; phenomenon, phenomena*

Finally, compound nouns must be considered individually. Depending on the sense, the *s* may be added to the whole expression or to the main word in the compound: *commander in chief, commanders in chief; sister-in-law, sisters-in-law; cupful, cupfuls; spoonful, spoonfuls; go-between, go-betweens; take-off, take-offs.* For other compounds, and for any other plurals about which you feel doubtful, you should consult your dictionary.

Possessive Forms

The term *possessive* for English nouns is sometimes misleading, but it is the term in common use. The possessive form may show ownership, but it often conveys other ideas. A few examples will suggest the range of the possessive:

Physical ownership:	*the woman's hat, Roger's house, the child's nose*
Action or feeling:	*the sergeant's command, John's anger, Helen's ambition*
Association:	*Drake's pursuers, the boy's defeat, her aunt's death*

| Measure: | *an hour's delay, a day's journey, a week's vacation* |
| Miscellaneous: | *yesterday's newspaper, duty's call, for pity's sake* |

Actually these constructions are similar in one respect: they are the equivalent of phrases with the preposition *of.* Compare: *the hat of the woman, the command of the sergeant, the pursuers of Drake, a delay of an hour,* etc. That is the test you should use when you put an *s* at the end of a word, to determine whether the sense is plural or possessive —or both.

The rules for forming the possessive are clear and rather simple:

Add an apostrophe and *s* to form the possessive of nouns that do not end in *s*, whether singular or plural: *the woman's hat, the women's hats, the child's nose, the children's noses.*

Add an apostrophe and *s* to form the possessive of most singular nouns ending in *s*; but if the second *s* makes the word difficult to pronounce, add only the apostrophe: *Bess's party, Thomas's friend, Mr. Jones's house, Dickens's novels* (or *Dickens' novels*), *Moses' staff, Jesus' parables, Socrates' philosophy.*

Add only the apostrophe to form the possessive of plural nouns ending in *s*: *the girls' dormitory, the sergeants' commands, the Scotts' garden, the Joneses' car.*

Possessive noun modifiers offer a special problem to grammarians. You can see why by comparing these three expressions:

his hat
the *man's* hat
the old *man's* hat

In the first expression we call *his* an adjective because it modifies *hat.* But if for the same reason we call *man's* an adjective, what shall we say about the word *old*? It must be an adjective modifying *man,* or *man's.*

About all we can do is to call *man's* a noun in the possessive case, even if we aren't being quite consistent. Every once in a while English grammar is not completely logical.

Practice in Recognizing Nouns

Pick out all nouns in the following sentences. (Answers on page 156)

1. We felt a series of strong shocks.
2. Our whole party reached the summit and returned before nightfall.
3. Through my binoculars I could see Camp Three on a ledge across the valley.
4. Daphne du Maurier wrote a book about her father.
5. My brother has not really recovered from his last attack of the flu.
6. There is only one way to discover the truth.
7. Has the ship reached the dock?
8. The ordinary small-town practitioner will suffer under this arrangement.
9. We shall never know what fears he suffers from.
10. One member of the group gave the leader a great deal of trouble.

Practice in Using Capital Letters

Insert capitals wherever needed. Be careful not to use unnecessary capitals. Example: In my last two years at college I
E
expect to major in ~~e~~nglish and history. (Answers on page 156)

1. During the summer we swam in long island sound.
2. We will be staying at the willard parker hotel on monday.
3. The northwest is the source of some of the main tributaries of the mississippi river.
4. The camp is about a mile to the east of the river.
5. The emancipation proclamation was signed during the third year of the civil war.

Practice in Forming Plurals and Possessives

For each of the following nouns write the plural, the possessive singular, and the possessive plural. Example: hero, heroes, hero's, heroes' (Answers on page 157)

1. secretary	6. son-in-law	11. chief	16. soprano
2. child	7. lady	12. monkey	17. wolf
3. woman	8. church	13. mosquito	18. deer
4. Negro	9. Englishman	14. alumnus	19. attorney
5. boy	10. fox	15. baby	20. policeman

PRONOUNS

Functions of Pronouns

Certain differences between nouns and pronouns were described in the previous chapter. Another point of difference is that nouns are practically unlimited; whenever anything new is discovered or invented, or a new idea introduced, we can create a noun for it: e.g., *television, existentialism, laser, turbojet.* Pronouns, on the other hand, are a fairly fixed group of words.

There are, however, a number of types and classifications. In the popular definition *a pronoun is a word that stands for a noun,* as in these sentences:

If Sam wants any tools, let *him* have *them.*

The man *who* washes the windows is here.

The pronouns *him, them,* and *who* stand for *Sam, tools,* and *man* respectively. In such relationships the noun is called the *antecedent* of the pronoun.

There are many pronoun uses to which the standard definition does not so obviously apply:

Who goes there?

Has *it* finally come to *this*?

Here the pronouns do not refer back to any clearly identified antecedents. However, in a sense the pronouns are serving in the place of nouns; that is, they fit into the sentences in places which nouns would normally fill, as subject, object of a preposition, etc.

The several major classes of pronouns must be examined separately, since each class has its special characteristics and problems.

Personal Pronouns

Person, as used in grammar, refers to the three possible subjects of speech: the person speaking (first person), the person spoken to (second person), and the person or thing spoken about (third person). The personal pronouns have different forms for the three persons, as well as for number, gender, and case.

Modern English uses the following forms:

	FIRST PERSON	SECOND PERSON	THIRD PERSON
SINGULAR			
NOMINATIVE	I	you	he, she, it
POSSESSIVE	my, mine	your, yours	his, her, hers, its
OBJECTIVE	me	you	him, her, it
PLURAL			
NOMINATIVE	we	you	they
POSSESSIVE	our, ours	your, yours	their, theirs
OBJECTIVE	us	you	them

Number is the characteristic that makes a word singular or plural. Nouns have certain rules for forming the plural, outlined in the previous chapter. The personal pronouns have radical changes in form, except in the second person, where singular and plural are identical.

Gender is significant only in the third person singular, where *he, his,* and *him* are masculine; *she, her,* and *hers* feminine; *it* and *its* neuter.

Case depends upon the use of a word in a sentence. Some uses of nominative and objective case forms are illustrated here:

NOMINATIVE CASE

SUBJECT

He is lonely. *They* knew what *they* wanted.

PREDICATE NOMINATIVE

It must have been *she.*

Was it *he* who told you?

Note: In the first person singular it has become customary to use the objective case form for this construction, except in very formal writing: It's *me.*

OBJECTIVE CASE

DIRECT OBJECT

Stanley knows *her*.   Have you seen *them*?

INDIRECT OBJECT

Give *him* your address. He showed *me* another route.

OBJECT OF A PREPOSITION

Are you coming with *me*?   Nothing can come between *us*.

Certain of the possessive forms (*my, our, your, her, their*), while commonly listed under pronouns, are never used as such. They are more properly considered as adjectives, since they are used only to modify nouns. These are possessive adjectives:

It was *my* choice.
I thought *her* essay was best.

These are possessive pronouns:

The choice is *mine*.   (predicate nominative)
I thought the best essay was *hers*.   (predicate nominative)
She took *theirs* by mistake.   (direct object)
I prefer his hat to *yours*.   (object of a preposition)
Your house is larger, but *ours* has more garden space.   (subject)

The possessive pronoun is also used in a kind of double possessive: a friend of *mine*; that car of *hers*.

The possessive case forms of personal pronouns, you will note, do not use apostrophes.

The personal pronoun *it* has some peculiar impersonal uses:

It's clearing up.
It may rain.
It's a beautiful day.
It's time to go.
It is useless to deny the accusation.

In some such sentences, like the last two, *it* is considered an expletive. (Compare with the expletive *there* in Chapter 3.)

Compound Personal Pronouns

Certain possessive and objective forms combine with the words *self* or *selves* to make compound personal pronouns: *myself, ourselves, yourself, yourselves, himself, herself, itself, themselves*. These forms have two uses, *reflexive* and *intensifying*.

The reflexive construction shows the action of a verb returning to the subject: I enjoyed *myself.* She hurt *herself.* They conducted *themselves* well. Behave *yourself.*

The intensifying construction is used for emphasis, and usually appears immediately after the noun or pronoun it emphasizes: I *myself* saw the accident. The captain *himself* didn't know what was happening. The car *itself* was undamaged.

The compound forms should be avoided in other constructions, where the regular pronoun will serve:

SUBSTANDARD: Harry and *myself* were present.
STANDARD: Harry and *I* were present.
SUBSTANDARD: The problem was referred to Sheila and *myself.*
STANDARD: The problem was referred to Sheila and *me.*

Relative Pronouns

The definite relative pronouns are *who, which,* and *that.* *Whom* is the objective case form of *who.*

These pronouns occur in constructions called *relative clauses.* A *clause* is a group of words containing a subject and a verb. A relative clause depends upon a word or words in the main clause:

The man *who stole the car* has been caught.

The man has been caught is the main clause. The relative clause is used as an adjective to modify the noun *man.* Notice that the relative pronoun *who* does double duty: it is the subject of *stole* in the relative clause; it also stands for the noun *man,* and connects the relative clause to this noun.

The choice of *who* or *whom* depends on its construction in the relative clause:

The man *whom you accused* is not guilty.
The policeman *to whom I spoke* was very helpful.

In these sentences the relative pronouns serve as objects, of the verb *accused* and of the preposition *to;* hence the objective form is used.

Whose, the possessive form of *who,* is commonly used as an adjective:

The woman *whose house I rented* is my cousin.

Whose modifies *house.*

The relative pronouns *which* and *that* are invariable and have no case changes:

The wind *that* comes in the spring . . . (subject)
The house *that* Jack built . . . (direct object)
The book to *which* he referred . . . (object of a preposition)

Who, which, and *that* are differentiated in meaning. *That* can be used for persons or things, but *who* (*whom, whose*) is used only for persons, and *which* never for persons. The older use of *which*, as in "Our Father, *which* art in heaven," is archaic.

In certain constructions the relative pronoun may be omitted:

The girl (whom) Harvey is engaged to was at the party.
Is that the dog (that) I saw in the yard?

Indefinite Relative Pronouns

The definite relative pronouns that you have been considering have antecedents in the main clause. However, relative pronouns are often used without antecedents, whence they are called *indefinite*. The common indefinite relative pronouns include the following: *who* (*whom, whose*), *which, what, whoever* (*whomever*), *whatever*.

The sentences below illustrate how this use differs from the definite use:

I can guess *whom* you're referring to.
I know *whose* it was.
What I think doesn't seem to matter.
Whoever comes will be welcome.
He does *whatever* he likes.

The relative clauses in these sentences are not used as adjectives; they are used as nouns. (A more extended treatment of clauses will be found in Chapters 18 and 19.)

Interrogative Pronouns

The forms *who* (*whom*), *which*, and *what* may introduce questions. When they do, they are called *interrogative pronouns*:

Who told you that story?
Whom has he selected?
Which do you prefer?
What is the fare to Chicago?

These are direct questions, followed by question marks. Interrogative pronouns are also used to introduce indirect questions:

I want to know *who* told you that story.

Interrogative pronouns, as you see, have no antecedents.

The distinction between nominative and objective forms is sometimes ignored in interrogative pronouns, but in formal speech or writing it should be maintained:

COLLOQUIAL: *Who* did you take to the party?
FORMAL: *Whom* did you take to the party?

Demonstrative Pronouns

The demonstrative pronouns are *this, that, these, those*—usually defined as pronouns which point out something. In speech they do not require antecedents:

Is *this* the last train?
Look at *that*!
I'll take *these*.
Those are too large.

In writing, the demonstrative pronouns may take antecedents, but there is no fixed rule. The pronoun may point forward:

This is my answer:

Or the reference may be quite general:

Those were the days.
That was too much for me.

The writer should merely make certain that the reference of the pronoun will be clear to the reader.

Demonstrative pronouns should not be confused with demonstrative adjectives, which are the same words in different constructions:

PRONOUN: *This* is my book. Are *those* the pictures you took?
ADJECTIVE: *This* book is mine. Did you take *those* pictures?

Indefinite Pronouns

The largest of the pronoun classes is that of indefinite pronouns:

Many are called, but *few* are chosen.
Somebody should help him.
Each of us has his own locker.

Since the one outstanding characteristic of these pronouns is a concern with number—singular or plural—they are listed here in three groups: those that indicate a single person or thing; those that indicate more than one; and those that indicate a portion or part of something. Some words belong to more than one group.

SINGULAR INDICATORS: anybody, anyone, anything, everybody, everyone, everything, somebody, someone, something, another, each, either, neither, nobody, nothing, none, one.

PLURAL INDICATORS: all, any, both, enough, few, more, none, plenty, several, some.

PORTION INDICATORS: all, any, enough, less, little, more, much, none, plenty, some. The portion indicators are singular, and are used with things that cannot be counted:

All of the time (gold, water, sand) *is* . . .

The plural indicators are used with things that can be counted:

All of the men (chairs, pencils, houses) *are* . . .

The importance of the distinctions indicated by this grouping becomes clear when the pronouns are used with verbs or with personal pronouns. The verb or the personal pronoun should agree in number with the indefinite pronoun:

Each of the guests had to show *his* ticket.
All of the guests had to show *their* tickets.
Neither of your figures *is* correct.
Both of your figures *are* correct.

Some of the indefinite pronouns have this similarity with nouns: that they form the possessive with an apostrophe:

One's manners reveal his upbringing.
Nobody's life is safe any more.
One should not infringe upon *another's* rights.

Reciprocal Pronouns

Two compound expressions, *each other* and *one another*, are called reciprocal pronouns, since they express a relationship back and forth. The two words in each expression are used together and considered as one pronoun:

They are fond of *each other*.
They are fond of *one another*.

As a rule the term *each other* suggests two; *one another* more than two.
The reciprocal pronouns also use the apostrophe for the possessive:

Bear ye *one another's* burdens.

Practice with Personal Pronouns and Adjectives

Underline every personal pronoun or adjective, and draw an arrow to the antecedent. Example: Everyone likes to feel that he is important. (Answers on page 157)

1. The boys complained that Myra had taken their skates.
2. No one should leave his seat without permission.
3. Each man naturally thinks of himself first.
4. Several customers accused the proprietor of cheating them.
5. If anyone wants the book, give it to him.
6. The height of the building is its chief distinction.
7. Both of the farmers succeeded in selling their hogs.
8. Everyone must have a good strong stick. He will need it in these woods.
9. Neither of those workers is worth his salt.
10. A girl can really enjoy herself at the lake.

Practice in Recognizing Uses of Pronouns

Find and underline every personal, relative, or interrogative pronoun. Write above it the appropriate letter or letters to indicate whether it is a subject (*S*), predicate nominative (*PN*),

direct object (*DO*), indirect object (*IO*), or object of a preposition
(*OP*).   Example: Is <u>he</u> the soldier to <u>whom</u> <u>they</u> gave the medal?
(Answers on page 158)

1. Give it to them if they ask for it.
2. Who told you that story?
3. How did he know whose it was?
4. I don't know who took the crullers.
5. To him that hath shall be given.
6. The leader may choose whomever he wishes.
7. The police promised leniency to whoever would confess.
8. She's going with the boy whom she met at the dance.
9. The package that I forgot to mail was for you.
10. What do you know about him?

Practice in Using Indefinite Pronouns

For each blank supply an indefinite pronoun which makes good
sense and which agrees with the following verb and/or pronoun in
number—singular or plural.   You may find that there are several
words which will work equally well.   (Answers on page 158)

1. _____ of the contestants has paid the same entry
fee.
2. _____ of the food has any flavor.
3. _____ of the workers have abandoned their right
to strike.
4. _____ who leaves his coat here must take his
chances.
5. I haven't spoken to _____ of the boys about his
marks.
6. I haven't spoken to _____ of the boys about their
marks.
7. _____ of the men aren't doing their share of the
work.
8. If _____ has his orders, we can get started.
9. _____ of the money seems to have disappeared.
10. _____ has any intention of avoiding his responsibilities.

APPOSITIVES

A noun or pronoun can be used in a construction called an *appositive*—a word or words *in apposition*. In the following the italicized expressions are appositives:

> At camp we met Mr. Willett, the *scoutmaster*.
> Our first dog, a *spaniel*, was very fond of the baby.
> The two senior members, *Stella and I*, are in charge of public relations.

Appositive means, in its origins, "placed next to." An appositive is a word or group of words usually occurring directly after another noun or pronoun, and standing for the same thing. *Scoutmaster* is in apposition with *Mr. Willett*, *spaniel* with *dog*, *Stella and I* with *members*.

An appositive or appositive phrase (which includes all modifying words) is usually set off by commas:

> The guide, a *man* of great courage and skill, was mainly responsible for our rescue.
> His trouble was money, the notorious *root* of all evil.

Dashes may be used when the appositive phrase is long, or is separated from its governing word:

> Only one passenger in the entire bus load—a tall, pale *gentleman* in clerical garments—seemed unperturbed by the incident.

A colon is often used to precede an appositive at the end of a sentence:

> We took only the bare essentials: *blankets, toilet kits*, a few *pots* and *pans*.

However, when the appositive is simple and very closely related to its governing word, no punctuation is used:

My friend *Bob* has a new car.
We *all* went to see it.
You *members* must give your support.
Shaw's play *Arms and the Man* is included in the anthology.

These are called *close* or *restrictive* appositives.

An appositive is in the same case as the word with which it is in apposition. This rule is meaningful with regard to personal pronouns:

There were only three absentees: you, Stanley, and *I*. (*absentees* is a predicate nominative; hence the nominative *I*)
The brunt of the punishment fell on the two guards, Stanley and *me*. (*guards* is object of the preposition; hence the objective *me*)

Practice in Recognizing Appositives

Underline each appositive, and draw an arrow to the word with which it is in apposition. Example: The weapon, an ancient stiletto, was lying in the ashes. (Answers on page 159)

1. My friend the blacksmith gave me a horseshoe.
2. The capital city, Halifax, is a major seaport, the western terminus of many passenger and freight ships.
3. It was decided that Dr. Loomis, a member of the faculty, should be asked to act as our spokesman.
4. There is a serious weakness in your whole scheme: lack of money.
5. You older boys can take my car, the Ford station wagon.
6. We sent a very diplomatic reply, one which should have pleased everybody.
7. Two of us, Harriet and I, are reading Le Carré's popular thriller, *The Spy Who Came In from the Cold.*
8. The whole Collins family—mother, father, and three children—piled into the back seat.
9. Most of the growers have decided to limit their efforts to two varieties: McIntosh and Delicious.
10. Your sister Jean has been dating a classmate of mine, Angus Robey.

14

ADJECTIVES

Kinds of Adjectives

An adjective is used to *modify* a noun or pronoun, that is, to describe the noun or pronoun or make its meaning more definite:

> by telling what kind: *yellow* flower, *large* building, *fast* car, *useless* venture
>
> by pointing out which one: *my* house, *his* sister, *this* room, *whose* pen
>
> by telling how much or how many: *both* hands, *several* minutes, *enough* rope, *more* time

The words that tell what kind are called *descriptive adjectives*. The other two groups, those that tell which one, how much, or how many, are called *limiting adjectives*.

As in the examples shown above, an adjective commonly appears before its noun. On occasion, for effective expression, it may follow the noun:

> A fragment of parchment, *yellow* with age, was spread out on the table.
>
> The sea, *deep* and *mysterious*, will hold its secret forever.

A *predicate adjective* (see page 26) is separated from the word it modifies by a verb:

> This man is *mad*.
> The fault was *mine*.
> The supplies were *adequate*.
> Marion looks *attractive*.
> He seems *happy*.

Descriptive adjectives are a very large group of words. In addition to the ordinary adjective forms, almost any noun can function on occasion as a descriptive adjective: *street* signs, *desk* blotter, *baggage* room, *idea* man, *philosophy* professor, *resistance* movement. These words do not have all the qualities of adjectives—they cannot be compared—but they do essentially the same job.

The *limiting adjectives* include a number of different types, almost all of which, with the exception of the articles (*a, an,* and *the*), are words that can also be used as pronouns (see Chapter 12):

POSSESSIVE ADJECTIVES: *our* garden, *her* gloves, *your* job

RELATIVE ADJECTIVES: the man *whose* name you mentioned; I know *what* time he came

INTERROGATIVE ADJECTIVES: *Which* house? *What* kind? *Whose* idea?

DEMONSTRATIVE ADJECTIVES: *this* gun, *that* number, *those* horses

INDEFINITE ADJECTIVES: *each* boy, *some* candy, *another* day, *either* parent

ARTICLES: *a, an, the.* *A* and *an* are the indefinite articles; *the* is the definite article. *A* is used before a word beginning with a consonant sound, *an* before a word beginning with a vowel sound: *a* clock, *a* yacht, *a* solemn oath, *an* eagle, *an* honest man, *an* ordinary day. (But: *a* useful gift, *a* one-mile run— since the initial sounds are the consonants *y* and *w*.)

Comparison of Adjectives

Most descriptive adjectives can be compared; that is, they can express degrees of a quality: positive, comparative, and superlative. There are two regular methods of comparison: with the endings -*er* and -*est*, and with the words *more* and *most*. Generally the first method is applied to the shorter and more commonly used adjectives, but there is no clear rule.

The following comparisons are fairly representative:

POSITIVE	COMPARATIVE	SUPERLATIVE
tall	taller	tallest
early	earlier	earliest
noble	nobler	noblest

friendly	friendlier	friendliest
strong	stronger	strongest
evil	more evil	most evil
alert	more alert	most alert
beautiful	more beautiful	most beautiful
famous	more famous	most famous

The present tendency of the language is to give easy acceptance to the *more-most* comparison. If there is any doubt you could say *more noble* or *more friendly* without fear of criticism; whereas *eviler* or *famouser* would be absurd and illiterate.

The use of both methods at the same time ("more stupider," "most fastest") would now be regarded as an ignorant error, although it was quite acceptable in the sixteenth century; e.g., "This was the most unkindest cut of all."

A few adjectives are compared irregularly:

bad	worse	worst
good	better	best
little	less	least
much, many	more	most
far	further	furthest
	farther	farthest

Further-furthest can be used for all purposes; *farther-farthest* only for physical distance: "It's just a few steps *further* (or *farther*)," "We have no *further* recommendations."

In careful use the superlative degree applies only when three or more things are being compared. For the comparison of two things, the comparative degree should be used:

Howard is certainly the *taller* of the two.

Although both drugs were tried, the doctors felt that penicillin was the *more effective*.

I've traveled frequently by plane as well as by ship, and I've always liked the ship *better*.

Another matter for careful expression involves adjectives which have an absolute quality, like *white, unique, perfect, dead, round*. These words are not literally capable of comparison: if a thing is really *white*, or *round*, or *unique*, it cannot become *whiter*, or *rounder*, or *more unique*. In practice, however, particularly where the sense is not quite literal, we do use expressions like "whiter than snow" or "the deadest town in the state."

Practice in Identifying Adjectives

Underline all adjectives (except articles); write *PA* above the predicate adjectives. Example: The next night was cold and
dismal. (Answers on page 159)

1. The new type seems simpler to operate.
2. We must take an accurate, realistic approach to every problem.
3. The female passengers were green with envy.
4. Stormy weather is predicted for a whole week.
5. A thick, wet, yellow fog settled over the harbor.
6. Fourteen cases of this deadly disease have been reported.
7. The local newsstand is owned by a blind veteran.
8. He was reluctant to cooperate with the newly-appointed supervisor.
9. Your generosity is overwhelming.
10. There should be a better method of dealing with hardship cases.

Practice in Distinguishing Adjectives from Pronouns

Underline and label adjectives (*A*) and pronouns (*P*). Example:
Now it's every man for himself. (Answers on page 159)

1. This seems to be the end of everything.
2. Many of my friends have taken your viewpoint.
3. Anyone who comes early will have several choices.
4. Don't pay any attention to what he says.
5. All members must bring their credentials to every meeting.
6. More time has been spent on this problem than it's worth.
7. There would be little advantage in our waiting another hour.
8. Which building did they rent for their new office?
9. Each of you knows something about that story.
10. They hardly speak to each other.

Practice in Comparing Adjectives

Give the preferred comparative and superlative degrees of the following words.   (Answers on page 160)

1. tiny	6. impossible	11. small	16. distinct
2. severe	7. dark	12. distant	17. fatal
3. adequate	8. good	13. careful	18. bottom
4. fast	9. brainy	14. awkward	19. timid
5. perfect	10. polite	15. narrow	20. wrong

ADVERBS

Functions of Adverbs

Adverbs are similar to adjectives in the fact that they modify other words in the sentence. Adverbs modify verbs, adjectives, or other adverbs.

Most adverbs modify verbs, in certain regular ways:

by telling how: They moved *swiftly*.
by telling when: They moved *immediately*.
by telling where: They moved *forward*.
by telling how much or to what extent: They moved *slightly*.

Adverbs may modify adjectives or other adverbs, usually telling how or to what extent:

with adjectives: *almost* six feet; *exactly* six feet
with other adverbs: *rather* awkwardly; *very* awkwardly

The function of an adverb, however, is not always easy to define. Some common adverbs (*possibly, indeed, however, not, therefore,* etc.) do not seem to answer the usual questions; nor do they always, as adjectives do, refer to specific words in the sentence:

He did *not* answer to his name.
Possibly the best route would be across the causeway.
It was *indeed* a disastrous venture.

In sentences like the last two, the adverb is sometimes said to modify the whole idea of the sentence rather than a particular word.

Forms of Adverbs

Many adverbs are formed from adjectives, by adding an *-ly* ending: *swift/swiftly, usual/usually, rough/roughly, delightful/delightfully,* *real/really, lawless/lawlessly, sincere/sincerely.* This is by no means a clear test of an adverb, however, for two reasons. (1) A number of adjectives end in *-ly*: *early, friendly, lowly, manly, kindly, portly*; (2) many common adverbs have a different form: *not, here, there, now, then,* etc. Certain other words have the same form whether used as adjectives or as adverbs:

ADJECTIVE	ADVERB
a *fast* train	it came *fast*
a *short* time	he stopped *short*
the *early* bird	he rose *early*
a *hard* worker	he works *hard*
a *close* decision	the car came *close*

A few such words have two adverb forms: *quick/quickly, slow/slowly, tight/tightly, cheap/cheaply.* The difference is in the degrees of formality: Drive *slow.* Advance *slowly.*

Position of Adverbs

Adverbs that modify verbs have no fixed position in the sentence:

Finally we reached a decision.
We *finally* reached a decision.
We reached a decision *finally.*
Slowly the great gate descended.
The great gate *slowly* descended.
The great gate descended *slowly.*

This gives the writer flexibility in placing his words for greatest effect.

When an adverb interrupts a verb phrase, it usually appears after the first word of the phrase:

He will *not* be offered another chance.
The accident might *easily* have been prevented.
The work has *so often* been interrupted that I'm beginning to despair.

With a few adverbs, shifting the position may alter the sense or clarity of the sentence:

Winifred *almost* passed all her courses. (almost passed)
Winifred passed *almost* all her courses. (almost all)

We *only* talked about the problem yesterday.   (we only talked)
We talked *only* about the problem yesterday.   (only about the problem)
We talked about the problem *only* yesterday.   (only yesterday)

Comparison of Adverbs

Most descriptive adverbs may be compared (see comparison of adjectives, page 6o).

Only a few, mostly those that have a form identical with adjectives, use the *-er* and *-est* endings: *fast, early, cheap, close,* etc.:

You'll have to move *faster*.
Evelyn came *closest* to having a perfect score.

Most *-ly* adverbs are compared with *more* and *most*:

The new office is located *more conveniently*.
The motor operates *most efficiently* in cold weather.
She dresses *most conservatively*.
He has contributed *most generously* to our campaigns.

As in the last two sentences, *most* sometimes has the force of *very*.

A few adverbs, like corresponding adjectives, are compared irregularly:

well	better	best
badly	worse	worst
far	farther	farther
	further	furthest
little	less	least
much	more	most

Adverbs and Adjectives Distinguished

The choice of an adverb or a predicate adjective after a verb depends on whether the modifier describes the action of the verb or the nature of the subject (after a linking verb):

Joyce looked *weary*.   (pred. adj.—*weary* describes Joyce)
Joyce looked *wearily* at the pile of letters.   (adv.—*wearily* describes how she looked at the letters)

The children were *happy*. (pred. adj.)
The children played *happily*. (adv.)

Good and *well* should be carefully differentiated. *Good* is always an adjective. *Well* is usually an adverb; but it is used as an adjective for certain meanings—attractive, satisfactory, in good health:

The dinner was *good*. (adj.)
Mrs. Klein looks *well* in that dress. (adj.)
All is *well*. (adj.)
He spoke *well*. (adv.)
The scarf goes *well* with that dress. (adv.)

Adverbs and Prepositions Distinguished

Many words that are commonly prepositions can be used as adverbs, the difference being that prepositions take objects and adverbs do not:

ADVERB	PREPOSITION
Mr. Price strolled *by*.	Mr. Price strolled *by* the house.
Don't look *down*.	Look *down* the valley.
Let's walk *around*.	Let's walk *around* the house.

Practice in Recognizing Adverbs

This exercise contains many of the adverbs which do not have the *-ly* ending to identify them. See if you can recognize and underline them all. Example: Don't you think you're going <u>too</u> <u>fast</u>? (Answers on page 160)

1. The job is almost finished.
2. Meanwhile the procession had passed by.
3. Take him away and scrub him well.
4. If you lean over you can see further.
5. Indeed your arguments are very plausible.
6. The neighbors often come around for tea.
7. We can never thank you enough.
8. The food is always good on Sundays.
9. Irma is not very well.
10. The new office is more convenient but less attractive.

Practice in Distinguishing Adverbs, Adjectives, and Prepositions

Label each of the italicized words to indicate whether it is an adverb (*Adv*), a predicate adjective (*PA*), or a preposition (*P*).

Example: You'll be *exhausted* when you get *through*.   (Answers on page 160)

                    PA   Adv

1. Sarah brandished a rolling pin *threateningly* in her brawny fist.
2. Come *in* and join us.
3. I'm *sure* there is more *in* the kitchen.
4. Helen seems *happier*, but she's working much *harder*.
5. Look *around carefully* and get your bearings.
6. Saul gazed *around* him *wonderingly*.
7. The work may be *hard*, but it pays *well*.
8. At camp the boys get *up* and go to bed *early*.
9. A little sloop was sailing *jauntily up* the bay.
10. The future looks *more hopeful* than it did.

PREPOSITIONS

Listing and Functions

In Chapter 6 the subject of prepositions and prepositional phrases was introduced, so that you might recognize these constructions in use.

Since all prepositions are not simple little words like *of*, *to*, *in*, and *for*, you will find it useful to refer to this list of words commonly used as prepositions:

about	behind	concerning	like	to
above	below	despite	near	toward
across	beneath	down	of	under
after	beside	during	off	underneath
against	besides	except	on	until
along	between	for	over	unto
among	beyond	from	past	up
around	but (meaning	in	since	upon
at	except)	inside	through	with
before	by	into	throughout	within
				without

Compound prepositions:

according to	because of	out of	owing to
alongside of	instead of	together with	up to

By definition, a preposition connects a noun or pronoun to some other word in a sentence. The whole prepositional phrase, then, acts as a modifier of this word, and may function as either an adjective or an adverb:

ADJECTIVE PHRASES	ADVERB PHRASES
one *of the boys*	run *with the ball*
the road *to town*	enter *through the window*
a piece *of cake*	think *of that*
men *against death*	high *in the sky*
house *in the country*	sitting *in the hammock*

As with single word modifiers, an adjective phrase usually occurs immediately next to the word it modifies. The position of an adverb phrase is not so restricted:

According to your story, Mansfield fell *off the roof into the yard*.

In this sentence the three prepositional phrases are all used as adverbs to modify the verb *fell*.

Should a Sentence End with a Preposition?

Many of the words listed as prepositions can also be used as adverbs (see page 67). As a rule you can easily tell the difference, since the preposition is followed by an object:

ADVERBS: I saw him passing *by*.   Look out *below*!
PREPOSITIONS: He passed *by* my window.   It was priced *below* cost.

Because of this distinction, there is a common belief that a sentence cannot properly end with a preposition. In normal use, however, with interrogative and relative pronouns, this idea doesn't hold true. In the sentences below, the forms at the left are more natural, hence more desirable, except in formal writing:

What shall I eat *with*?	*With what* shall I eat?
What port did he sail *from*?	*From what port* did he sail?
Which door did you come *through*?	*Through which door* did you come?
Whom are you voting *for*?	*For whom* are you voting?
. . . book (*which*) you were talking *about* . . .	. . . *about which* you were talking . . .
. . . a man (*whom*) you can depend *on* . . .	. . . *on whom* you can depend . . .

Before starting on the practice exercise, it might be a good idea to refer to the warning about infinitives on page 19.

Practice in Identifying Prepositional Phrases

In the following sentences draw parentheses around every prepositional phrase, label it *Adj* or *Adv*, and draw an arrow to the word it modifies. Example: Most (of the new buildings) are equipped (with air conditioning). (Answers on page 161)

1. Henry looked around for the owner of the shop.
2. We stood on the steps and waited patiently for a chance to look inside.
3. The children from the neighborhood gazed at us in amazement.
4. With one exception the members of the committee were satisfied.
5. Beneath his rugged exterior he has a heart of gold.
6. Throughout the play I had an impression of impending doom.
7. Pamela likes to read books about travel and adventure.
8. The two cars raced through the main street and headed for the open country.
9. The shelves were loaded with a collection of old leather volumes with stained and ragged covers.
10. During the night in the cave, Rudolph gained tremendous respect for his native friends.

CONJUNCTIONS

A *conjunction* is a word whose primary function is to join words or groups of words. Unlike prepositions, conjunctions are used in a great variety of situations; in fact, an understanding of the proper uses of conjunctions can be of great help in the writing of clear, well-constructed sentences.

Conjunctions are of two main types: *coordinating conjunctions* (which include *correlative conjunctions*) and *subordinating conjunctions*.

Coordinating Conjunctions

As the name suggests, coordinating conjunctions are normally used to connect sentence elements of the same grammatical class: nouns with nouns, adverbs with adverbs, clauses with clauses:

> Their only weapons were scythes *and* pitchforks. (nouns)
> Some of them hesitated *and* started to retreat. (verbs)
> Dorothy is often moody *or* irritable. (adjectives)
> Slowly *but* steadily the speed increased. (adverbs)
> The sleigh was driven over the river *and* through the woods. (prepositional phrases)
> They seldom win, *yet* they keep on trying. (clauses)
> I liked the salesman, *so* I gave him a good order. (clauses)

If three or more items are being connected in a series, the conjunction need not be repeated:

> The course includes algebra, plane geometry, solid geometry, *and* trigonometry.
> His hat might be anywhere: behind the door, under the bed, *or* on the chandelier.

The words used as coordinating conjunctions are *and, but, or, nor, for, yet,* and *so.* The conjunction *nor* is not normally used by itself; it is part of the correlative *neither . . . nor.*

Correlative Conjunctions

The coordinating conjunctions *and, but, or,* and *nor* are often used with *both, not only, either,* and *neither,* respectively, to form what are known as *correlative conjunctions.* Correlatives are always used in pairs.

Notice that these, like the other coordinating conjunctions, join elements of the same class: nouns with nouns, verbs with verbs, etc.:

Both Democrats *and* Republicans will back such a proposal. (nouns)
Your method is *not only* wasteful *but* (*also*) slow. (adjectives)
Starkey *neither* drinks *nor* smokes. (verbs)
That clock runs *either* too fast *or* too slow. (adverbs)
Either the coffee is weak *or* you've added too much cream. (clauses)

Usually the meaning is practically the same as it would be with a simple coordinating conjunction, but there is an additional degree of emphasis:

He added sugar *and* cream.
He added *both* sugar *and* cream.

Subordinating Conjunctions

Subordinating conjunctions are used to connect adverb or noun (subordinate) clauses to some sentence element in a main clause. They do not connect adjective clauses, which are introduced and joined by relative pronouns (see page 51).

These are some of the words commonly used as subordinating conjunctions: *when, because, if, though, after, unless, until, whether, that.* (A more complete list is given in Chapter 19.)

Adverb clauses are used like adverbs, usually to modify verbs. The following sentences contain adverb clauses, introduced by subordinating conjunctions:

The flight was postponed *because* the pilot had a toothache.
Try it once more *before* you give up.

We'll miss the last bus *if* we don't hurry.
Vincent will fail his tests *unless* he does some serious study.
It looks *as if* it might rain.

Note that the adverb clause may precede the main clause:

When the bell rings, you'll see a mad rush.
After he left, I found his briefcase on the sideboard.

Noun clauses are used like nouns, most commonly as objects or predicate nominatives. The following sentences contain noun clauses, introduced by subordinating conjunctions:

He thinks *that* no one else can do the job.
Nobody knows *where* the coffee pot is.
You must decide *whether* the reward is worth the effort.
The question is *how* we can control him.

Some of the words used as subordinating conjunctions can also be used as prepositions. The same is true of the coordinating conjunctions *but* and *for*. Compare:

As I predicted, Sam is causing trouble again. (conjunction)
He has served three terms *as* captain. (preposition)

I haven't seen Barkus *since* his barn was burned down. (conjunction)
I haven't seen Barkus *since* Tuesday. (preposition)

They're willing enough, *but* they need more practice. (conjunction)
You seem to have everything *but* the kitchen sink. (preposition)

Practice in Recognizing Coordinating Conjunctions

Underline the coordinating conjunctions, including correlatives, in the following sentences. Tell whether they are being used to connect nouns, verbs, adjectives, adverbs, (prepositional) phrases, or clauses. Example: Give me liberty or give me death. (clauses)
(Answers on page 161)

1. The day dawned clear and cold. ( )
2. She agrees completely, or at least she says so.
   ( )

3. They are not only willing but anxious to help.
   (   )
4. Our men were fighting on land, at sea, and in the air.
   (   )
5. He should be at school or near it by this time.
   (   )
6. We looked grimly at each other, but no one said a word.
   (   )
7. Vote early and often.   (   )
8. She has good judgment, intelligence, and integrity.
   (   )
9. The trees are budding, yet the air still feels like winter.
   (   )
10. For days she neither slept nor ate.
    (   )

Practice in Recognizing Subordinating Conjunctions

Underline the subordinating conjunctions in the following sentences, and put parentheses around the subordinate clauses. Example: We haven't had any trouble with the car (since we left home.)
(Answers on page 162)

1. Unless I'm much mistaken, she is Mrs. Hamilton's niece.
2. Do it because I say so.
3. We can't start dinner until all the guests arrive.
4. Where were you when the fire broke out?
5. If the weather continues like this, we should have a good season.
6. After all the hunters were asleep, a dark figure stole through the camp.
7. Our lives are more complicated because we have more possessions.
8. Though we had little strength left, we decided to press forward.
9. When the bell rings, don't stop for anything.
10. I can't fasten the snap unless you keep still.

KINDS OF SENTENCES; CLAUSES

Kinds of Clauses

A clause is a group of related words containing a subject and a verb.   The following are all clauses:

> I prefer the later train
> . . . which leaves at three o'clock.
> Close the door
> . . . when you go out.

They are of two types: *main* (or independent) *clauses* and *subordinate* (or dependent) *clauses.*

A main clause expresses a complete thought and may constitute a sentence:

> I prefer the later train.
> Close the door.

A subordinate clause is not complete in itself; it must always be attached to some element in a main clause:

> I prefer the later train, *which leaves at three o'clock.*
> (The subordinate clause modifies the noun *train.*)
> Close the door *when you go out.*
> (The subordinate clause modifies the verb *close.*)

A subordinate clause may be a noun clause, an adjective clause, or an adverb clause.   The different types are discussed in the next chapter.

Kinds of Sentences

Sentences may be classified according to structure, depending on how many clauses they contain, and whether the clauses are main or subordinate.

A *simple sentence* contains one main clause and no subordinate clause:

> Mr. Filbert lost his wallet on the train.
> The explosion destroyed every house on the block.
> Who's in charge here?

A *compound sentence* consists of two or more main clauses. Each main clause in the following sentences is italicized:

> *The rains descended* and *the floods came.*
> *Penny has a new doll,* but *she still prefers the old one.*
> *The table lay on its side, several chairs were broken,* and *the floor was covered with slivers of glass.*

The main clauses in a compound sentence are usually connected by coordinating conjunctions (see page 73).

A sentence with a compound subject or a compound predicate may still be a simple sentence. Only when each verb has a separate subject do we have more than one clause:

> Mr. Filbert has lost his wallet and is very much upset. (simple sentence)
> Mr. Filbert has lost his wallet, and the whole family is upset. (compound sentence)

A *complex sentence* contains at least one subordinate clause in addition to a main clause. Main clauses in the following sentences are italicized; subordinate clauses are in parentheses:

> *The man* (who came to dinner) *stayed for several months.*
> *He gave me his solemn promise,* (which he promptly broke).
> (If you need me for anything), *press the white button.*
> *I'll join you* (after I've changed my clothes).
> *He wonders* (why we don't follow his plan).
> *I know* (what you mean).
> *I knew* (what you meant) (when you said it).

A *compound-complex sentence* is simply a combination of the last two. It contains two or more main clauses and at least one subordinate clause:

> *I know* (what you mean), but *I don't agree.*
>
> (Although the party ended fairly early), *there was a mess to clean up*, so *we didn't get to bed till two o'clock.*
>
> *Mr. Hankin is retired now*, and *the business* (that he founded) *is managed by his son-in-law.*

In examining the clauses in a sentence, you will note that each clause contains a subject and a verb. In the last sentence above, for example, there are three subjects and three verbs: *Mr. Hankin is retired; business . . . is managed; he founded.*

Practice in Recognizing Kinds of Sentences

In the following sentences underline all main clauses, put parentheses around all subordinate clauses, and classify each sentence as simple, compound, complex, or compound-complex. Example: <u>Study the situation carefully</u> (before you make your decision). (complex) (Answers on page 162)

1. A slight sound behind him brought him to his feet.
   (   )
2. The idea that you suggest seems brilliant.
   (   )
3. He advanced to the platform on which Bentley was standing.
   (   )
4. When you've had such an experience, you may recover but you'll never be the same. (   )
5. I don't know what I can say. (   )
6. By the middle of the afternoon we had given up all hope of rescue. (   )
7. All of his shirts looked as if they had been slept in.
   (   )
8. Take a cup of flour and work it into the mixture until it is thoroughly blended. (   )
9. The grass must be mowed before the sun is too hot.
   (   )
10. Not only have you burned my toast but you've spoiled my appetite. (   )

19

MORE ABOUT SUBORDINATE CLAUSES

A subordinate clause serves in place of an adjective, an adverb, or a noun:

AS AN ADJECTIVE
The food is distributed to the *neediest* families.
The food is distributed to the families *that need it most.*

AS AN ADVERB
You ought to come *early.*
You ought to come *before the other guests arrive.*

AS A NOUN
I heard his *comment.*
I heard *what he said.*

It is clear that the subordinate clause in each sentence is a unit, serving as a single part of speech.

Adjective Clauses

An adjective clause regularly follows the noun or pronoun that it modifies.

As a rule an adjective clause is introduced by one of the common relative pronouns, *who,* (*whom*), *which,* or *that* (see relative pronouns, page 51).   Hence it is called a *relative clause:*

I know a man *who owns one.*
He is a man *whom everyone admires.*
The rifle *of which you speak* never belonged to me.
The garden *that surrounds the house* is overgrown with weeds.

In many sentences the relative pronoun can be omitted, particularly when it is the object of a verb or a preposition:

> The man *she married* couldn't support her. ("whom she married")
> Everybody *I speak to* seems to agree. ("to whom I speak")
> The picture *I showed you* is a Vermeer. ("that I showed you")
> The route *he took* is a little shorter. ("that he took")

Relative clauses may be introduced by the relative adjective (*whose*) or the relative adverbs (*when, where,* and *why*):

> A man *whose life is at stake* may use desperate measures.
> We have eight members *whose dues have not been paid.*
> I know a place *where the wild thyme grows.*
> This is a time *when everyone must search his conscience.*

Adverb Clauses

An adverb clause usually appears just before or just after the main clause:

> *If the weather is too unpleasant,* we'll postpone the picnic.
> We'll postpone the picnic *if the weather is too unpleasant.*

> *Until he actually admitted his guilt,* I believed him innocent.
> I believed him innocent *until he actually admitted his guilt.*

> *When you finish,* take the dirty dishes to the kitchen.
> Take the dirty dishes to the kitchen *when you finish.*

Most adverb clauses, as in the foregoing sentences, modify the key word in the main clause, the verb. However, certain adverb clauses may modify adjectives or adverbs:

> You are later *than I expected.*
> Finish your homework *as* quickly *as you can.*

These constructions have some unusual features, which will be explained below under "Clauses of Comparison."

Adverb clauses have a wide range of uses. Awareness of this range will help you to recognize adverb clauses and to use them more effectively. The following list illustrates some of the most common types, with the principal conjunctions:

CLAUSES OF TIME (*when, before, after, until, since, while*)
Before you go, turn off the radio.
It is only six months *since the bill was signed.*

CLAUSES OF PLACE (*where, wherever*)
Put the gun *where the children can't find it.*
I'll go *wherever he sends me.*

CLAUSES OF MANNER (*as, as if, as though*)
Everything worked out *as he expected.*
We must behave *as if everything were normal.*

CLAUSES OF CAUSE (*because, since, as*)
Because we couldn't get the motor running, we had to row back to
    the dock.
Since no one else will volunteer, I'll do the cooking.

CLAUSES OF CONCESSION (*although, though, while*)
While the large universities have many advantages, I still prefer a
    small college.
Although she uses only two fingers, she is a very fast typist.

CLAUSES OF CONDITION (*if, unless*)
I'll drop in later *if anything new comes up.*
Unless the traffic is very bad, we should arrive by eight.

CLAUSES OF RESULT (*so, so that, so . . . that*)
We knew about their plans, *so we were ready for them.*
It looked *so* stormy *that we decided to stay home.*

CLAUSES OF PURPOSE (*so, so that, in order that*)
Clear the doorway *so that the others can enter.*

CLAUSES OF COMPARISON (*as . . . as, so . . . as, than*)
The clause of comparison is different from all the other types
    of adverb clause in two respects: (1) It is used to modify an
    adjective or an adverb rather than a verb.   (2) It may be
    elliptical; that is, some words in the clause may not be ex-
    pressed (words in parentheses in the following sentences).

Your book isn't *as* long *as mine* (*is*).
A turkey costs more *than a chicken* (*does*).
Do you need George any more *than* (*you do*) *me?*

Do you need George any more *than I* (*do*)?
It's more difficult *than it seems*.
Come *as* quickly *as you can*.

These clauses, especially in the elliptical construction, are sometimes difficult to distinguish from prepositional phrases. Bear in mind that *as . . . as* and *than* are conjunctions.

Noun Clauses

Noun clauses are most common in the position after the verb, as predicate nominatives or direct objects. They may, however, be used in any normal noun function:

SUBJECT OF A VERB
What he needs is a complete rest.
Whatever you decide is satisfactory to me.

WITH THE EXPLETIVE "IT"
A noun clause may appear at the end of a sentence, introduced by the expletive *it*. In this construction, which is fairly common, the noun clause is considered the subject of the verb. Compare:

Where he gets his supply is not generally known.
It is not generally known *where he gets his supply*.

That her mother was there was unfortunate.
It is unfortunate *that her mother was there*.

PREDICATE NOMINATIVE
My feeling is *that the boy is innocent*.
That was *why I waited*.

OBJECT OF A VERB
I know *what you're thinking*.
Can you explain *how the accident happened*?

OBJECT OF A PREPOSITION
Give it to *whoever needs it*.
He worries about *how his business will be affected*.

APPOSITIVE (see Chapter 13: Appositives)
The noun clause in apposition is a fairly common construction, but it must be carefully distinguished from an adjective clause modifier. Compare:

The argument *that he presented* was not convincing. (adjective clause)

His final argument, *that women are more inclined to violence,* was not convincing. (noun clause)

The subordinate clause in the first sentence describes or identifies the word *argument* (*that* is a relative pronoun); in the second sentence the clause *is* the argument (*that* is a subordinating conjunction). Similarly:

You have ignored one fact *that is very important.* (adjective clause)

You have ignored the fact *that some insects are useful.* (noun clause)

The most common connective for a noun clause is the conjunction *that.* Others are *what, which, if, whether, who, whom, when, where, whoever, whatever.*

Identifying Main and Subordinate Clauses

In a complex sentence with an adjective or adverb clause, the separation of the two clauses is relatively easy:

I admire a man *who has convictions.*
We can start *whenever you're ready.*

In analyzing such sentences it is customary to say that *who has convictions* and *whenever you're ready* are subordinate clauses; and that *I admire a man* and *We can start* are main clauses.

Some grammarians prefer to consider all modifiers, even clause modifiers, of any word in the main clause as parts of the main clause. By this interpretation the subordinate clauses would still be as we have indicated; but the main clause, in each of the sentences cited, would be the entire sentence.

The advantage of this approach becomes obvious as we consider sentences with noun clauses:

What he needs is a complete rest.
My feeling is *that the boy is innocent.*

Since, by definition, a main clause expresses a complete thought, it would be rather absurd to say that the main clauses in these sentences are *is a complete rest* and *My feeling is*; especially in the former instance, where the main clause would lack a subject.

Of course this is merely a matter of terminology. Work on the assumption that a main clause cannot always be considered separately from the subordinate noun clause.

Practice in Identifying Adjective and Adverb Clauses

The following sentences contain adjective and adverb clauses. Put parentheses around each subordinate clause, label it Adjective or Adverb, and draw an arrow to the word that it modifies. Example: (As he turned to face the crowd), I recognized the man (who had held the gun).   (Answers on page 162)

1. The evil that men do lives after them.
2. The only thing we have to fear is fear itself.
3. Until Mr. Kinnick arrived, nothing happened.
4. The second half of the test is easier than the first half.
5. She is always in a state of expectation when the postman brings a letter.
6. Until he was in his fifties, Mr. Steiner lived in Austria, where he was a famous chef.
7. When the drought had lasted for about three weeks, the water supply became dangerously low.
8. We were annoyed by the billboards, which obscured most of the scenery.
9. Since you obviously disapprove, why don't you resign?
10. She always sends me a note if I miss anything that seems important.

Practice in Identifying Noun Clauses

The following sentences contain noun clauses. Put parentheses around each noun clause and label it subject (S), predicate nominative (PN), object of a verb (OV), object of a preposition (OP), or appositive (Ap). Example: You do (whatever you want to do). (Answers on page 163)

1. I believe that a stronger argument could be made.
2. It was known that Honeywell was prejudiced.
3. Does he know where you went?

4. According to what he says, the polls cannot be taken seriously.
5. The consensus was that the plan should be abandoned.
6. What you're saying is that people change.
7. The fact that a statesman is also a politician doesn't detract from his statesmanship.
8. It is true that certain requirements must be met.
9. Whoever made the statement is misinformed.
10. I never worry about what I can't help.

20

A DICTIONARY OF GRAMMATICAL TERMS

Abstract Noun. A noun that names a quality or a concept, something that cannot be perceived by the senses: *love, enjoyment, direction, emptiness.* See p. 43.

Action Verb. As distinguished from Linking Verb, a verb that tells what the subject is doing: *go, see, lose, repeat,* etc. See p. 24.

Active Voice. The form of the verb used when the subject is thought of as acting rather than receiving an action. Compare Passive Voice. See p. 35.

Adjective. A word used to describe or limit a noun or a pronoun. See p. 59.

Adjective Clause. A subordinate clause used as an adjective. See p. 79.

Adjective Phrase. A prepositional phrase used as an adjective. See p. 70.

Adverb. A word used to describe or limit a verb, an adjective, or another adverb. See p. 64.

Adverb Clause. A subordinate clause used as an adverb. See p. 80.

Adverb Phrase. A prepositional phrase used as an adverb. See p. 70.

Adverbial Conjunction. See Conjunctive Adverb.

Adverbial Objective (or Adverbial Noun). A noun used as an adverb, to modify a verb, an adjective, or an adverb:

I saw him *yesterday.*

Saul came home *last night.*

We walked three *miles.*

Agreement. Grammatical correspondence between two parts of speech. A verb agrees with its subject in person and number. A pronoun agrees with its antecedent.

Antecedent. A noun or noun-equivalent to which a following pronoun refers. Certain personal, relative, and demonstrative pronouns have antecedents. See p. 48.

Apostrophe. The mark (') used in contractions and possessive forms. See p. 46.

Appositive. An explanatory noun or pronoun, usually placed immediately after the noun or pronoun with which it is in apposition. See p. 57.

Article. A group term for the words *a* and *an* (indefinite articles) and *the* (definite article). They are usually considered a kind of subcategory of adjectives.

Auxiliary. Part of a verb used with another verb form in a verb phrase. See p. 11.

Being Verb. See Linking Verb.

Case. The property of a noun or a pronoun which indicates its relation to other words in the sentence, such as that of subject or object. See Nominative, Objective, Possessive.

Clause. A group of related words containing a subject and verb with their modifiers. See p. 76.

Close Appositive. An appositive so closely allied to the noun or pronoun with which it is in apposition that no comma is used between them: *my brother Sam, the planet Mars.*

Collective Noun. The name of a group of beings or things: *crowd, family, collection.*

Colloquial. A term applied to speech or writing that is informal.

Common Noun. As distinguished from Proper Noun, a name applied to a group or a member of a group, rather than to an individual: *boy, dog, city, river.*

Comparative Degree. The form of an adjective or adverb that expresses *more* of a quality, with the word *more* or the suffix *-er*: *higher, slower, more charming, more quietly.* See p. 60.

Comparison. The change in the form of an adjective or adverb to express a quality (Positive), more of a quality (Comparative), or most of a quality (Superlative). See p. 60.

Complement. That part of the predicate used after the verb to complete the meaning. See p. 15.

Complete Predicate. The verb plus all its modifiers and complements. See p. 9.

Complete Subject. The simple subject plus all its modifiers. See p. 9.

Complex Sentence. A sentence containing one main clause and at least one subordinate clause. See p. 77.

Compound-Complex Sentence. A sentence containing two or more main clauses and at least one subordinate clause. See p. 78.

Compound Personal Pronoun. A personal pronoun with the suffix *-self* or *-selves*. In use it is either Intensive or Reflexive. See p. 50.

Compound Predicate. A predicate composed of two or more verbs, usually joined by a coordinating conjunction. See p. 13.

Compound Preposition. A preposition consisting of two or more words: *out of, according to.*

Compound Sentence. A sentence composed of two or more main clauses. See p. 77.

Compound Subject. A subject composed of two or more nouns or pronouns, usually joined by a coordinating conjunction. See p. 13.

Concrete Noun. The name of a thing or class of things that can be perceived by the senses: *calendar, man, flower, smile, hammer, jolt.* See p. 43.

Conjugation. The inflectional forms of a verb used to indicate person, number, tense, voice, and mood.

Conjunction. A word used to join other words or groups of words. There are two principal kinds of conjunctions, Coordinating and Subordinating. See p. 72.

Conjunctive Adverb. An adverb which has an additional function as a connective between clauses, or between sentences: *therefore, however, moreover, nevertheless, hence, consequently.* It is often used after a semicolon.

Contraction. The shortening of a word or phrase by the omission of one or more letters in the middle. In writing, contraction is indicated by the apostrophe, as in *don't, can't, it's, you're.*

Coordinating Conjunction. A conjunction that connects two sentence elements of equal rank, as distinguished from the Subordinating Conjunction. See p. 72.

Copulative Verb. Another term for Linking Verb.

Correlative Conjunctions. Coordinating conjunctions that are used in pairs: *both . . . and, either . . . or, neither . . . nor.* See p. 73.

Declarative Sentence. A sentence that makes a statement. See p. 6.

Declension. The inflectional forms of a noun or pronoun, to show case and number.

Definite Article. See Article.

Degree. See Comparative Degree, Superlative Degree.

Demonstrative Adjective. A type of limiting adjective that points out: *this* house, *that* corner, *these* apples. See p. 60.

Demonstrative Pronoun. A pronoun that points out: *This* is the boy. See p. 53.

Dependent Clause. Another term for Subordinate Clause.

Descriptive Adjective. An adjective that describes the noun it modifies, as opposed to a Limiting Adjective. See p. 59.

Direct Address (Nominative of Address). A noun naming a person or persons addressed, not related grammatically to other elements in the sentence:

Did you bring the flowers, *Pamela?*

Friends, Romans, countrymen, lend me your ears.

Direct Object. A complement which occurs after a transitive verb, to complete the meaning. See p. 25.

Ellipsis (Elliptical Expression). The omission of a word or words when the context makes the meaning clear: A chisel would work better than a plane *(would work).*

Emphatic Form. A name commonly used for the form of a verb with the auxiliaries *do, does,* or *did: Do try* a little harder. You may not believe us, but we *did see* him.

Exclamatory Sentence. A sentence which expresses strong feeling. It is often different in word order from the other kinds of sentences:

What a beautiful day!

How silly!

See p. 6.

Expletive. It or *there* used merely to precede the verb where the real subject follows the verb. See pp. 10 and 82.

Finite Verb. Any complete verb form, as distinguished from a verbal.

Future Perfect Tense. The tense formed with the auxiliaries *will have* or *shall have* (passive *will have been* or *shall have been*). It is used to express an action preceding another action in the future.

Future Tense. The tense, formed with *will* or *shall,* used to express action in the future.

Gender. The grammatical expression of sex distinctions. In English it affects only the third person singular pronouns *he, she,* and *it.*

Gerund. A verbal ending in *-ing*, used as a noun. It is sometimes called a verbal noun or a noun participle. See p. 41.

Gerund Phrase. A gerund with any complement or modifiers.

Idiom. An expression peculiar to a language, depending on custom rather than logic: *It's raining. Can you tell time? I give up.*

Imperative Mood. A form of a verb used for commands. See Mood.

Imperative Sentence. A sentence in which the verb is in the imperative mood. The subject is usually *you* understood. See p. 6.

Impersonal "It." A term used for the vague use of the pronoun *it* in such sentences as "It's raining" or "It's time to go." See p. 50.

Indefinite Adjective. A word like *some, both, any, many, either, several,* used to modify a noun:

> *Many* hands make light work.
>
> *Several* books have disappeared.
>
> Have you *any* matches?

See p. 60.

Indefinite Article. See Article.

Indefinite Pronoun. A word like *some, both, any, many, either, several,* used in a noun construction as subject, object, predicate nominative, etc.:

> *Many* are called, but *few* are chosen.
>
> *Either* will do.

See p. 54.

Indefinite Relative Pronoun. A relative pronoun that introduces a noun clause and has no antecedent in the main clause. See p. 52.

Independent Clause. Another term for Main Clause.

Indicative Mood. A form of a verb used for statements or questions. See Mood.

Indirect Object. A word that follows a verb and tells to or for whom something is done. It is in turn followed by a direct object, expressed or implied. See p. 26.

Infinitive. A verbal, usually preceded by *to*, and used as a noun, an adjective, or an adverb. See p. 39.

Infinitive Phrase. An infinitive with complement and modifiers.

Inflection. Changes in the form of a word to indicate changes in meaning or in use. The inflection of nouns and pronouns is called declension. The inflection of verbs is called conjugation.

Intensive Pronoun. One type of Compound Personal Pronoun, in which the suffix *-self* is used to intensify the meaning: The principal *himself* congratulated me. She did it *herself.* See p. 51.

Interjection. An exclamatory word that has no grammatical relationship with the rest of the sentence: *whoops, ouch, alas.* See p. 21.

Interrogative Adjective. A word that introduces a question and also modifies a noun: *Whose* desk is it? *Which* club did you use? See p. 60.

Interrogative Adverb. A word that introduces a question and also modifies a verb, adjective, or adverb: *When* did he leave? *Why* are all the lights on?

Interrogative Pronoun. A word that introduces a question and also functions in place of a noun: *Who* is responsible for this? *Which* of them is more reliable? *What* did he say? See p. 52.

Interrogative Sentence. A sentence that asks a question. See p. 6.

Intransitive Verb. A verb that has no object: *Wait* for me. She *has been studying* hard. See p. 16.

Irregular Verb. A verb that forms its past tense or past participle other than by the simple addition of *-d* or *-ed*. Many of the common English verbs, like *do, go, make, tell, write, speak,* are irregular. See p. 28.

Limiting Adjective. An adjective that merely points to or identifies or limits its noun, instead of describing it. See p. 60.

Linking Verb. A verb that links its subject to a predicate nominative or a predicate adjective. The most common linking verb is *be.* Others are *become, seem, appear, look, taste,* etc. See p. 24.

Main Clause. A clause that is complete in itself, not subordinated to some other grammatical construction. In a simple sentence the main clause and the sentence are identical. See p. 76.

Modal Auxiliary. As distinguished from the common auxiliaries, which are usually forms of *be* or *have,* the modal auxiliaries add to the principal verb an idea such as necessity, obligation, permission, etc. The forms frequently used are *can, could, may, might, must, shall, should, will, would.*

Modifier. Usually an adjective or an adverb. Any word or group of words used to describe or limit another word or group of words.

Mood. The attitude of the speaker toward the sentence, whether indicative (making a statement), imperative (giving a command), or subjunctive (posing an unreal or hypothetical situation).

Nominative. The case name for the subject of a sentence or a predicate nominative. See p. 49.

Nominative Absolute. A phrase consisting of a participle (or some equivalent construction) plus a subject of the participle: *the dishes done, his face contorted with rage.* It is called *nominative* because the subject is in the nominative case; and *absolute* because it has no clear grammatical connection with the rest of the sentence:

> *His face contorted with rage,* Mooney stalked out of the chamber.
> *I being the elder,* they all looked accusingly at me.
> *Dinner being over,* we had four empty hours ahead of us.

Nonrestrictive. A term for a modifier that describes but does not limit or identify the word it modifies. A nonrestrictive modifier, since it is parenthetical, is set off by commas. See Restrictive.

> My father, *who was celebrating his birthday,* was feeling very gay.
> The Steuben Library, *which has its own system of cataloging,* is not participating in the study.
> Kaufman, *irritated by the delay,* expressed himself forcibly.
> We finally tabled the motion, *realizing that we could not agree.*

Noun. A word used to name a person, a place, a thing, a quality, or an action. See p. 43.

Noun Clause. A subordinate clause used as a noun. See p. 82.

Number. A property of nouns, pronouns, and verbs, that indicates whether the reference is to one (singular) or more than one (plural).

Object. A noun or noun-equivalent that follows and is governed by a transitive verb or a preposition.

Objective. The case name for an object of a verb or a preposition. See p. 50.

Objective Complement. A noun or an adjective that follows an object and is necessary to complete its meaning:

> We painted the barn *white.*
> We made Charley the *chairman.*
> He finds physics *difficult.*

Parenthetical. A term applied to a word or expression appearing in a sentence but not necessary for the essential thought or the structure. It may be set off by parentheses, but commas or dashes are more usual:

> Our financial condition, *however,* has never been better.
> A swimming pool, *you know,* needs a lot of attention.
> Certain grammatical taboos—*e.g., the split infinitive*—are no longer so frightening.

Participle. A verbal used as an adjective. See Present Participle and Past Participle.

Participle (Participial) Phrase. A participle with its complement or modifiers.

Parts of Speech. The eight classes into which words are grouped according to function: *verb, noun, pronoun, adjective, adverb, preposition, conjunction,* and *interjection.* See p. 21.

Passive Voice. The form of the verb that tells what is done to the subject rather than what the subject does. Compare Active Voice. See p. 35.

Past Participle. A verbal used as an adjective and expressing past time. In form it often ends in *-ed,* sometimes in *-en;* but there are several dozen verbs in which the form is quite irregular: *talked, failed, suspected, taken, eaten, burnt, gone, caught.* Also one of the Principal Parts of a verb, used with auxiliaries to form the passive voice and the perfect tenses. See pp. 28, 41.

Past Perfect Tense. A tense consisting, in its simple form, of the auxiliary *had* (passive voice *had been*) plus the past participle form of a verb. It is used to express time prior to some other past time. See p. 35.

Past Tense. The tense form commonly used to express action at some point in the past. The past tense is included as one of the principal parts of a verb. See p. 33.

Perfect Tense. One of three tenses (see Present Perfect, Past Perfect, Future Perfect) formed with a past participle preceded by the auxiliaries *have* or *has, had,* or *will have.*

Person. The grammatical property of verbs and personal pronouns which indicates whether a person is speaking (first person), spoken to (second person), or spoken about (third person). See p. 49.

Personal Pronoun. A pronoun with inflectional changes to indicate the three possible persons and singular or plural number. See p. 49.

Phrase. A group of related words, as Verb Phrase, Prepositional Phrase, Participle Phrase, Gerund Phrase, Infinitive Phrase.

Plural. The classification of number that indicates more than one. See Number.

Positive Degree. The basic form of an adjective or adverb. See Comparison.

Possessive. The case form of nouns and pronouns that indicates ownership or some equivalent association. See p. 45.

Possessive Adjective (Possessive Pronoun). A personal pronoun used as a possessive modifier. See p. 50.

Predicate. The verb in a sentence, with all complements and modifiers. The predicate comprises what is said about the subject.

Predicate Adjective. An adjective used as a predicate complement after a linking verb, modifying the subject. See p. 26.

Predicate Complement. A noun, a pronoun, or an adjective used to complete the meaning of a linking verb and to identify or modify the subject. See p. 25.

Predicate Nominative. A noun or pronoun used as a predicate complement after a linking verb and identifying or representing the subject. See p. 25.

Predicate Noun. See Predicate Nominative.

Preposition. A word that relates a noun or pronoun (its object) to some other word in a sentence. See p. 69.

Prepositional Phrase. A preposition plus its object. Prepositional phrases commonly function as adjectives or adverbs. See p. 18.

Present Participle. A word made from a verb, ending in *-ing*, and functioning as a verbal modifier of a noun or pronoun; or, as one of the principal parts, it may be used with auxiliaries to form verb phrases. See pp. 28, 41.

Present Perfect Tense. A tense consisting, in its simple form, of the auxiliary *have* or *has* (passive voice *have been* or *has been*) plus the past participle. It is used generally to express time in a period in the past stretching up to the present. See p. 35.

Present Tense. The form of the verb used to express present time. See p. 33.

Principal Clause. See Main Clause.

Principal Parts. The basic verb forms from which all other verb forms may be derived. In this book the parts listed are present, past, present participle, and past participle. See p. 28.

Progressive Tenses. Verb forms occurring in all six tenses, which show the action as going on at the time indicated. In the active voice the progressive tenses are formed by adding a part of the verb *be* to the present participle. See p. 32.

Pronominal Adjective. See Possessive Adjective.

Pronoun. A word used instead of a noun in one of the noun functions (subject, object, etc.). See p. 48.

Proper Noun. The name of an individual person, place, or thing. Proper nouns are capitalized. See p. 43.

Reciprocal Pronoun. A pronoun that expresses mutual relationship: *each other, one another.* See p. 55.

Reflexive Pronoun. A term for an object that names the same person or thing as the subject: She blames *herself.* He hurt *himself.* See Compound Personal Pronoun.

Regular Verb. A verb that forms its past tense and past participle by the addition of *-d* or *-ed*: *please/pleased, talk/talked, growl/growled.*

Relative Adjective. A word that introduces a subordinate (relative) clause and functions as an adjective within the clause:

> He looks like a man *whose* conscience is clear.

See p. 60.

Relative Adverb. A word that introduces a subordinate (relative) clause and functions as an adverb within the clause:

> I know the shop *where* you bought that hat.

See p. 80.

Relative Clause. A subordinate clause introduced by a relative pronoun, a relative adjective, or a relative adverb. See p. 79.

Relative Pronoun. A pronoun that introduces a subordinate clause and functions as a pronoun within the clause. The common forms are *who, whom, which, that, what.* See Indefinite Relative Pronoun; also p. 79.

Restrictive. A term for a modifier which is necessary for the meaning of the sentence. Such a modifier is generally not set off by commas. See Nonrestrictive.

> The only fan *that works* is in the bedroom.
>
> A man *who can't pull his weight* is useless on this job.
>
> I can't drink coffee *without sugar.*

Restrictive Appositive. Same as Close Appositive.

Retained Object. An object that is kept in its object position following the verb when the verb is put into a passive voice form:

> Active: They gave us a choice.
>
> Passive: We were given a *choice.* (*choice* is a retained object)

Sentence Modifier. An adverb used to modify the essential idea of a sentence rather than the verb:

> *Fortunately,* he died painlessly.
>
> *Of course,* you aren't the only one.

Simple Sentence. A sentence containing a single main clause and no subordinate clause. See p. 77.

Singular. That classification of number which indicates only one. See Number.

Split Infinitive. A construction in which a word, usually an adverb, occurs between *to* and the verb form: *to really succeed.* See p. 40.

Subject. A word or group of words about which something is said by the predicate. See pp. 3 and 9.

Subjective Complement. Another term for Predicate Complement.

Subjunctive Mood. The mood of a verb used to express a wish or a condition contrary to fact. See p. 36.

Subordinate Clause. A clause functioning as a noun, an adjective, or an adverb, being thus dependent on or subordinate to something else in the sentence. See p. 76.

Subordinating Conjunction. A conjunction used to join a subordinate clause, except a relative clause, to a main clause. See p. 73.

Substantive. A term applied to any word or group of words used as a noun. It may be a noun, a pronoun, an infinitive, a gerund, or a clause.

Superlative Degree. The form of an adjective or adverb that expresses most of a quality, with the word *most* or the suffix *-est*: *highest, prettiest, most ornate, most vigorously.* See p. 60.

Tense. That property of a verb which indicates the time of the action. There are six tenses, in both simple and progressive forms: present, past, future, present perfect, past perfect, and future perfect. See p. 32.

Transitive Verb. A verb that has an object: *Take* this letter. I *can't see* his face. See p. 16.

Verb. A word or a group of words that says something about the subject. See p. 9.

Verbal. A word made from a verb but functioning as a noun, an adjective, or an adverb. A verbal may be a participle, a gerund, or an infinitive. See these terms; also p. 39.

Verb Phrase. A group of words used together as a single verb: *was going, has seen, has been stolen, will be rested.* See p. 10.

Voice. The form of a verb which indicates whether the subject acts (active voice) or is acted upon (passive voice).

Harry *painted* that picture. (Active)

That picture *was painted* by Harry. (Passive)

Part II
PUTTING GRAMMAR TO WORK

In this section you will be able to apply your knowledge of English grammar obtained in the first half of the book. Each chapter begins with a listing of the background materials which provide a basis for the explanations and exercises in the chapter. You may wish to go back over parts of this "background" first; or you may refer to it now and then as occasion requires.

Remember that the practical value of a knowledge of grammatical principles is their effect in improving your speech and writing. Here you will actually be "putting grammar to work."

MAKING VERBS AGREE

Background

Recognition of simple subjects (Chapter 3)
Compound subjects (Chapter 4)
Prepositional phrases (Chapter 6)
Singular and plural forms of verbs (Chapter 9)
Singular and plural forms of nouns (Chapter 11)
Singular and plural forms of indefinite pronouns (Chapter 12)

Basic Grammar

A verb should agree in number (singular or plural) with its subject:

SINGULAR	PLURAL
He goes	They go
He takes	They take
He prefers	They prefer
He maintains	They maintain

Note that the singular form of a verb ends in *s* in the third person.

Putting It to Work

1. In order to decide whether you need a singular or a plural verb, you must first find the subject and determine whether it is singular or plural.

2. Don't be confused by prepositional phrases or other elements coming between the subject and its verb:

WRONG: A box of crayons *were* lying on the table.
RIGHT: A box of crayons *was* lying on the table.

WRONG: So many witnesses testifying to his innocence *makes* our case look bad.

RIGHT: So many witnesses testifying to his innocence *make* our case look bad.

WRONG: The principal, as well as three of the teachers, *have* taken an interest.

RIGHT: The principal, as well as three of the teachers, *has* taken an interest.

RIGHT: The principal and three of the teachers *have* taken an interest.

3. Always use a plural verb with the pronoun *you*:

WRONG: I thought you *was* first on the list.
RIGHT: I thought you *were* first on the list.

4. Don't be confused by contractions; expand them if necessary. *Don't* is a contraction of *do not* and is consequently plural:

WRONG: She *don't* want to come.
RIGHT: She *doesn't* want to come.

WRONG: It looks like rain, *don't* it?
RIGHT: It looks like rain, *doesn't* it?

5. Don't be confused by the expletive *there*, or any other construction in which the subject follows the verb:

WRONG: *There's* only six rooms in the house.
RIGHT: *There are* only six rooms in the house.

WRONG: In a box on the counter *was* a cat and two kittens.
RIGHT: In a box on the counter *were* a cat and two kittens.

6. Make the verb agree with the subject, not with the predicate nominative:

WRONG: His main concern *are* the problems of his constituents.
RIGHT: His main concern *is* the problems of his constituents.
RIGHT: The problems of his constituents *are* his main concern.

7. A compound subject with the conjunction *and* is plural, except in special instances where the nouns are so closely related that they comprise a single idea:

WRONG: A white dress and a brightly colored handbag *makes* a striking combination.

RIGHT: A white dress and a brightly colored handbag *make* a striking combination.

but RIGHT: Bread and butter *is* all he wants.

8. A compound subject with *or* or *nor* (*either . . . or, neither . . . nor*) is singular if both parts are singular, plural if both parts are plural; but if only one part is plural, the verb agrees with the nearer part:

WRONG: Either Harriet or Doris *are* welcome to come, but not both at once.

RIGHT: Either Harriet or Doris *is* welcome to come, but not both at once.

WRONG: Neither the players nor the coach *feel* very confident.

RIGHT: Neither the coach nor the players *feel* very confident.

9. Use singular verbs with these indefinite pronouns and adjectives: *one, anyone, everyone, anybody, everybody, nobody, each, every, either, neither*:

WRONG: Neither of his teachers *sympathize* with his ambitions.

RIGHT: Neither of his teachers *sympathizes* with his ambitions.

WRONG: Everybody in the crowd *were* wildly enthusiastic.

RIGHT: Everybody in the crowd *was* wildly enthusiastic.

WRONG: Each of you *have* a part to play.

RIGHT: Each of you *has* a part to play.

10. In a relative clause the pronoun (*who, which, that*) may be singular or plural, depending upon its antecedent. Find the antecedent before selecting the verb in the relative clause:

WRONG: It's one of those shaggy-dog stories that never *seems* to end.

RIGHT: It's one of those shaggy-dog stories that never *seem* to end. (*That* stands for stories and is consequently plural.)

11. Be careful in the use of nouns that are plural in form but singular in meaning.

Usually singular: *economics, ethics, mathematics, physics, news, mumps, measles*

Usually plural: *athletics, scissors, trousers, wages*

RIGHT: The news from abroad *is* rather grim.

RIGHT: Measles sometimes *has* serious consequences.

RIGHT: The scissors (a pair of scissors) *were* right in the drawer.

12. Be careful in the use of nouns with unusual singular and plural forms:

Singular: *alumna, alumnus, bacterium, datum, phenomenon*
Plural: *alumnae, alumni, bacteria, data, phenomena*

RIGHT: One alumnus *has* already written a letter of protest.

RIGHT: The data *have* been gathered from many sources.

13. Expressions of quantity and sums of money are usually regarded as units and take a singular verb:

RIGHT: Three years *is* a long time to be separated from one's friends.

RIGHT: Sixty miles an hour *is* the new speed limit on the turnpike.

RIGHT: Five dollars *seems* very reasonable for that shirt.

Practice in Making Verbs Agree

Select the correct form from the choices given in parentheses. (Answers on p. 164)

1. Neither of those chairs (*is, are*) safe to sit on.
2. There (*wasn't, weren't*) more than twenty people in the audience.
3. A pile of ragged suitcases and untidy bundles (*was, were*) waiting for us on the dock.
4. Mr. Buffle's new car (*doesn't, don't*) use much gasoline.
5. One significant political force in these states (*is, are*) the older retired people.
6. This is one of those changing communities that (*has, have*) developed entirely new problems.
7. About six million dollars (*has, have*) been made available for scholarships.
8. Your scissors (*needs, need*) sharpening.
9. Each of the new members (*receives, receive*) private instructions from the hostess.
10. Either the potatoes or the meat (*has, have*) a peculiar taste.

11. Physics as well as mathematics (*requires, require*) skill in abstract logic.

12. In such a situation there (*doesn't, don't*) seem to be any alternative.

13. A flowing white shawl and a hat with a tall feather (*completes, complete*) the ensemble.

14. Neither you nor he (*has, have*) any voice in the decision.

15. Our chief hope today (*is, are*) the men and women with broader vision.

16. Is it true that you (*was, were*) in a prison camp?

17. Every one of the rooms (*has, have*) cross ventilation.

18. There (*is, are*) only twenty-three dollars left in the treasury.

19. Henrietta is one of the best swimmers that (*has, have*) ever graduated from this school.

20. Either Collins or Steinbugler always (*calls, call*) the signals.

21. Anyone with a head for figures (*is, are*) welcome to work with us.

22. (*Here's, Here are*) your skates.

23. Strawberries and cream (*was, were*) the only dessert.

24. (*There's, There are*) some important news waiting for you at home.

25. A library full of current magazines and books (*provides, provide*) interest for guests on rainy days.

26. Twenty feet of hose (*isn't, aren't*) nearly enough.

27. You (*wasn't, weren't*) supposed to be here so early.

28. Neither of your friends (*seems, seem*) to enjoy the swimming.

29. This is one of those storms that (*blows, blow*) over very quickly.

30. Professor Pine with his wife and three daughters (*is, are*) arriving on today's train.

MAKING VERB FORMS ACCURATE

Background

Irregular verbs; principal parts (Chapter 9)
Note on *shall* and *will* (Chapter 9)

Basic Grammar

Irregular verbs usually have different forms for the past tense and the past participle. Confusion of these forms leads to errors. As an easy rule of thumb, bear in mind that the past tense form is never used with auxiliaries; the past participle, whenever it is used as a verb, must have auxiliaries.

PAST	PAST PARTICIPLE
He *went*	He has *gone*
I *spoke*	I have *spoken*
They *saw*	They have *seen*

Certain verbs having similar appearance or similar meaning, or both, must be carefully distinguished.

For correct speaking and writing, certain distinctions are still preserved between *shall* and *will*. *Will* is now in common use for most purposes; but *shall* should be used in the first person for polite questions offering a choice.

Putting It to Work

1. Guard against the vulgar use of a past participle where you need the past tense. The following forms, used as verbs, must have auxiliaries: *begun, done, drunk, rung, seen, sung, sunk.*

WRONG: He *done* what he could.
RIGHT: He *did* what he could.
RIGHT: He *has done* what he could.

WRONG: Harry *seen* the bus coming.
RIGHT: Harry *saw* the bus coming.
RIGHT: Harry *has seen* the bus coming.

2. Guard against the vulgar use of the past tense where you need a past participle. The following forms never take an auxiliary: *began, broke, chose, drank, flew, froze, went, rode, rang, shook, swam, took, tore, wrote.*

WRONG: We *were* almost *froze* during the night.
RIGHT: We almost *froze* during the night.
RIGHT: We *were* almost *frozen* during the night.

WRONG: Several passengers *were* badly *shook* up.
RIGHT: Several passengers *were* badly *shaken* up.

WRONG: *Has* he *went* without us?
RIGHT: *Has* he *gone* without us?
RIGHT: *Did* he *go* without us?

3. Take care to avoid confusion between the verbs *lie* and *lay*. They are easily confused, and many people use them incorrectly. The following forms are correct:

lie: recline, rest, remain inactive
    Present: The cards *lie* (*are lying*) on the table.
    Future: The cards *will lie* on the table.
    Past: The cards *lay* on the table.
    Perfect Tenses: The cards *have lain* (*had lain, will have lain*) on
                   the table.
(Note: *Lie* never takes an object.)

lay: put, place, set down
    Present: The player *lays* (*is laying*) his cards on the
                   table.
    Future: The player *will lay* his cards on the table.
    Past: The player *laid* his cards on the table.
    Perfect Tenses: The player *has laid* (*had laid, will have laid*) his
                   cards on the table.
(Note: *Lay* always takes an object.)

4. Distinguish carefully between other pairs of confusing verbs. The following forms are correct:

accept (receive): He *accepted* my apology.

except (leave out): Can we *except* one man from the general pardon? (*except* is most often a preposition)

affect (influence): The dampness *affects* my throat.

effect (bring about): The arbitrator *effected* a successful agreement. (*effect* is most often a noun)

borrow (take on loan): May I *borrow* your pen?

lend (give on loan): Will you *lend* me your pen?

bring (carry toward something): Please *bring* it here.

take (carry away): *Take* it to the library.

can (be able to): *Can* you swim across the lake?

may (have permission to): *May* I use your phone? (*may* also expresses possibility: It *may* rain)

leave (go away, abandon): *Leave* the room.   *Leave* it here.

let (permit): *Let* him go.   *Let* us pray.

set (put, place): *Set* the lamp on the table.   (*set* takes an object)

sit (be situated): *Sit* in the easy chair.   (*sit* does not take an object)

5. Don't confuse the adjective or preposition *past* with the verb *passed*:

RIGHT: They *passed* my door quickly.

RIGHT: They ran *past* my door.

6. Don't confuse the present form *lead* with the past and past participle *led*:

RIGHT: They *lead* an easy life these days.

RIGHT: They *led* an easy life last summer.

(The metal *lead*, which rhymes with *led*, is partly responsible for this confusion.)

7. Use *shall* instead of *will* for the future tense in first personal questions which offer a choice to the person asked. The following are correct in current usage:

Shall I talk to Martha? (choice)
Will I know Martha when I see her? (possibility)
Shall I take the train back? (choice)
Will I be able to get a train back? (possibility)

Practice in Supplying Parts of Irregular Verbs

Fill in the past tense and the past participle by repeating to yourself the words at the head of the column. (Answers on p. 164)

	PRESENT	PAST Yesterday I	PAST PARTICIPLE I have
1.	begin		
2.	break		
3.	bring		
4.	choose		
5.	come		
6.	do		
7.	draw		
8.	drink		
9.	drive		
10.	eat		
11.	fall		
12.	fly		
13.	forget		
14.	freeze		
15.	go		
16.	lay		
17.	lead		
18.	lie		
19.	run		
20.	see		
21.	shake		
22.	sink		
23.	swear		
24.	tear		
25.	write		

Practice in Selecting Correct Verb Forms

Select the correct form from the choices given in parentheses. (Answers on p. 164)

1. He might have (*broke, broken*) his neck on that apparatus.
2. Rover was (*laying, lying*) peacefully under the table.
3. Do you think Steerforth will (*accept, except*) the position?
4. Something has (*went, gone*) wrong with this typewriter.
5. (*Shall, Will*) we all stop in and have a soda?
6. Maizie would have (*drank, drunk*) the whole quart.
7. (*Can, May*) I look at the sports section for a moment?
8. Ken tells me you (*saw, seen*) the President.
9. The table was (*laid, lain*) for eight people.
10. The quartet (*sang, sung*) three encores.
11. Yesterday we (*laid, lay*) on the beach too long and were badly burned.
12. (*Shall, Will*) the office be open at nine o'clock?
13. (*Set, Sit*) that big vase on the floor by the fireplace.
14. The guide (*lead, led*) us through a narrow path in the underbrush.
15. Why don't you (*leave, let*) me concentrate on my work?
16. When you go, (*bring, take*) this package and leave it at the laundry.
17. Mother was deeply (*affected, effected*) by our dog's death.
18. With so much to do, the day (*passed, past*) very quickly.
19. The chops in the refrigerator were (*froze, frozen*) solid.
20. (*Shall, Will*) I get you a cushion for that chair?

23

PUTTING VERBS IN THE RIGHT TENSE
AND MOOD

Background

Tense forms of verbs (Chapter 9)
Subjunctive mood (Chapter 9)
Tense forms of infinitives (Chapter 10)
Subordinate clauses and connectives (Chapter 19)

Basic Grammar

The time element in grammar is expressed by six simple tenses and six progressive tenses.

The infinitive has two tense forms, present and perfect, which bear different time relationships to the main verb.

"Sequence of tense" refers to the logic of using the same tense or different tenses in several clauses. "Shift of tense" is any illogical or unnecessary change from one tense to another.

The subjunctive *were* is used to express conditions contrary to fact.

Putting It to Work

1. In ordinary narrative either the past tense or the historical present may be used, but not both in the same context. Don't shift tenses:

> WRONG: When I *reach* for the ball I *feel* something snap in my shoulder, and my arm *went* limp.
>
> RIGHT: When I *reach* for the ball I *feel* something snap in my shoulder, and my arm *goes* limp.
>
> RIGHT (and generally preferable): When I *reached* for the ball I *felt* something snap in my shoulder, and my arm *went* limp.

> WRONG: I *knew* that none of our neighbors *are* interested.
> RIGHT: I *knew* that none of our neighbors *were* interested.

2. In a subordinate clause that follows the main clause, use the present tense for a general truth, regardless of the tense in the main clause:

> WRONG: He often *cited* the ancient proverb that honesty *was* the best policy.
> RIGHT: He often *cited* the ancient proverb that honesty *is* the best policy.

> WRONG: Medieval man *was* not aware that the earth *was* round.
> RIGHT: Medieval man *was* not aware that the earth *is* round.

3. The change in point of view from direct discourse (exact quotation) to indirect discourse may require a change in tense. The following sentences are correct:

> Direct: Mr. Coleman says, "I don't like olives."
> Mr. Coleman said, "I don't like olives."
> Indirect: Mr. Coleman *says* that he *doesn't* like olives.
> Mr. Coleman *said* that he *didn't* like olives.

4. In expressing past time, distinguish between past tense, to indicate a point of time in the past, and present perfect, to cover a spread of time up to the present:

> RIGHT: He *spoke* to me yesterday about it. (past)
> RIGHT: He *has spoken* to me about it several times. (present perfect)
> RIGHT: *Did* you *finish* before dinner? (past)
> RIGHT: *Have* you *finished* yet? (present perfect)

5. Use the past perfect to indicate a past action earlier in time than some other past action:

> WRONG: Suddenly I realized that I *forgot* the tickets.
> RIGHT: Suddenly I realized that I *had forgotten* the tickets.

> WRONG: When the fuse blew, we knew that we *connected* the terminals wrong.
> RIGHT: When the fuse blew, we knew that we *had connected* the terminals wrong.

6. Avoid *would have* in a subordinate clause after *if*. Use the past perfect:

> WRONG: If you *would have been* in the audience, I would have seen you.
> RIGHT: If you *had been* in the audience, I would have seen you.

> WRONG: If they *would have played* fair, we might have won.
> RIGHT: If they *had played* fair, we might have won.

7. Use the perfect infinitive (*to have gone*, etc.) only to express action completed earlier than that of the main verb. For the normal sequence of tense, use the present infinitive:

> WRONG: We planned *to have gone* sailing with you.
> RIGHT: We planned *to go* sailing with you.

> WRONG: I should have liked *to have seen* you in that costume.
> RIGHT: I should have liked *to see you* in that costume.
> RIGHT: I should like *to have seen* you in that costume.

8. Use the subjunctive form *were* in contrary-to-fact statements after *if* and verbs expressing a wish:

> WRONG: If I *was* Mary, I'd take the job.
> RIGHT: If I *were* Mary, I'd take the job.

> WRONG: You speak as if you *was* my father.
> RIGHT: You speak as if you *were* my father.

> WRONG: Sometimes I wish he *was* making less money.
> RIGHT: Sometimes I wish he *were* making less money.

Practice in Choosing the Right Tense and Mood

Select the correct form from the choices given in parentheses. (Answers on p. 165)

1. We intended (*to drive, to have driven*) the whole distance in one day.
2. Blandish could have foreseen this if he (*had, would have*) planned more carefully.
3. If you (*was, were*) in the Army now, you wouldn't feel so independent.

4. Last night my friends and I (*decided, have decided*) to stay in town for the summer.

5. Lord Drummond sat staring at me grimly for a full minute before he finally (*speaks, spoke*).

6. We realized that might (*doesn't, didn't*) always make right.

7. If the team (*won, had won*), we would have celebrated.

8. Miss Perkins said that she (*doesn't, didn't*) want to discuss the matter.

9. Suddenly we (*catch, caught*) sight of the prisoner that (*escaped, had escaped*), and Stella (*screams, screamed*) frantically.

10. If he (*was, were*) a few inches taller, he'd be one of the best centers in the league.

11. Carver swaggered up to the plate and (*looks, looked*) at the pitcher with a confident smile.

12. I was very sorry (*to hear, to have heard*) of your accident.

13. Members of the club (*collected, have collected*) almost five hundred dollars in the past three years.

14. Mrs. Gordon said that she (*wants, wanted*) more time to think it over.

15. We heard on the radio tonight that several torpedo boats (*attacked, had attacked*) an American destroyer.

16. I would have come if you (*had, would have*) called me.

17. Aunt Polly expected (*to meet, to have met*) us at the bus terminal.

18. Of course we knew that crime (*doesn't, didn't*) pay.

19. By the time the police arrived at the scene, the rioters (*dispersed, had dispersed*).

20. The speaker announced that the meeting (*is, was*) called to order.

21. Don't you wish you (*was, were*) back at camp?

22. When we reached the dock, we (*see, saw*) the ship just pulling away.

23. If the weather (*had cleared, would have cleared*) after lunch, we might still have gone ahead with the hike.

24. I'm sure the neighbors would have been happy (*to hear, to have heard*) that we were moving.

25. Sue came in and wanted to know whether all the guests (*arrived, had arrived*) yet.

CHOOSING THE RIGHT CASE FOR PRONOUNS

Background

Objects of prepositions (Chapter 6)
Complements: predicate nominatives and objects (Chapter 8)
The gerund as a noun (Chapter 10)
Forms of personal and relative pronouns (Chapter 12)
Relative clauses (Chapter 19)
Elliptical clauses (clauses of comparison) (Chapter 19)

Basic Grammar

There are three "cases" in English: *nominative, objective,* and *possessive.* Certain pronouns have different forms for the three cases:

	NOMINATIVE (as subject)	OBJECTIVE (as object)	POSSESSIVE (as possessive pronoun or adjective)
PERSONAL PRONOUNS	I	me	my, mine
	you	you	your, yours
	he	him	his
	she	her	her, hers
	it	it	its
	we	us	our, ours
	they	them	their, theirs
RELATIVE PRONOUNS	who	whom	whose
	whoever	whomever	whosever

Putting It to Work

1. Use the nominative case for subjects and predicate nominatives:

WRONG: *Me* and Henry have plans for Saturday.
RIGHT: Henry and *I* have plans for Saturday.

WRONG: How did you know it was *her*?
RIGHT: How did you know it was *she*?

In the predicate nominative construction, the objective case is often accepted colloquially, particularly in the first person: It's *me*. That was *us*.

2. Use the objective case for objects of verbs, direct or indirect, and objects of prepositions:

RIGHT: They told *us* about *her*.

3. Don't be confused by compound constructions. Many common errors can easily be avoided if each part of a compound is tested separately:

WRONG: You and *him* can handle the job.
RIGHT: You and *he* can handle the job.   (you can; he can)

WRONG: They were planning a party for Mary and *I*.
RIGHT: They were planning a party for Mary and *me*.   (for Mary; for me)

WRONG: The chairman appointed Paul and *I* to serve as tellers.
RIGHT: The chairman appointed Paul and *me* to serve as tellers.   (appointed Paul to serve; appointed me to serve)

4. In elliptical clauses following *than* or *as . . . as*, test the case of the pronoun by supplying the omitted words:

RIGHT: You have a better record than *I* (have).
RIGHT: He'd rather take you than (take) *me*.
RIGHT: We don't expect to do as well as *they* (do).

5. Use possessive (modifying) rather than objective forms with gerunds:

WRONG: Do you object to *me* being present?
RIGHT: Do you object to *my* being present?

WRONG: There isn't a chance of *us* getting tickets.
RIGHT: There isn't a chance of *our* getting tickets.

In such sentences the gerund is the object of the preposition, and the pronoun is a modifier, not an object.

6. Don't use apostrophes in possessive personal pronouns or adjectives:

RIGHT: That canoe is *ours*.
RIGHT: The dog has lost *its* way.
RIGHT: *Whose* dog is it?

Apostrophes with pronouns indicate contractions: *it's = it is; who's = who is.*

7. Don't be confused by the position of a relative or interrogative pronoun.   Examine the structure of the clause in which it appears:

WRONG: That's the officer *who* Jack admires.
RIGHT: That's the officer *whom* Jack admires.   (*whom* is the object of *admires*)

WRONG: Give the hammer to *whomever* needs it.
RIGHT: Give the hammer to *whoever* needs it.   (*whoever* is the subject of *needs*; the noun clause *whoever needs it* is the object of *to*)

8. Don't be confused by a parenthetical expression, like *he says* or *you know*, standing between the relative or interrogative pronoun and its verb:

WRONG: That's the girl *whom* he says is his cousin.
RIGHT: That's the girl *who* he says is his cousin.   (who . . . is his cousin)

WRONG: *Whom* do you think ought to win?
RIGHT: *Who* do you think ought to win?   (who . . . ought to win)

9. Don't use an emphatic pronoun form (*myself, himself*, etc.) when an ordinary personal pronoun is adequate:

WRONG: Cyril and *myself* did most of the painting.
RIGHT: Cyril and *I* did most of the painting.

Practice in Determining the Case of Pronouns

Select the correct form from the choices given in parentheses. (Answers on p. 165)

1. (*Who, Whom*) did you say you saw at the movies?
2. If it was (*he, him*), why didn't you say so?
3. (*Whoever, Whomever*) you select will be satisfactory to me.
4. Corey and (*you, yourself*) are the logical candidates.
5. Are you surprised at (*us, our*) being here so early?
6. There's enough pie left for you and (*she, her*).
7. That's one woman (*who, whom*) I admire thoroughly.
8. The key should be returned to either John or (*me, myself*).
9. Between you and (*I, me*), they shouldn't be here at all.
10. They won at least two more games than (*we, us*).
11. It might be (*she, her*) (*who, whom*) made that phone call.
12. (*Who's, Whose*) car is that in front of the house?
13. I'm sorry for (*whoever, whomever*) takes that job.
14. She hasn't had as much experience as (*I, me*).
15. Mr. Lyman told Paul and (*I, me*) to work out the averages.
16. Our neighbor's cat has been having trouble with (*its, it's*) teeth.
17. (*Who, Whom*) do you know in Newport?
18. Mrs. Starr is the woman (*who, whom*) I believe offered her house for the reception.
19. I can't understand (*him, his*) making such a mistake.
20. If you had known (*who, whom*) he was, would you have been as cordial?
21. I know several girls who are prettier than (*she, her*).
22. (*Its, It's*) obvious that the dog knows (*its, it's*) master.
23. They'll probably appoint (*whoever, whomever*) makes the best score on Saturday.
24. I suspect you and (*I, me*) are the scapegoats.
25. When I heard that bellowing voice, I knew it must be (*he, him*).

25

MAKING PRONOUNS AGREE WITH ANTECEDENTS

Background

Recognition of simple subjects (Chapter 3)
Compound subjects (Chapter 4)
Personal pronouns: person, number, and gender (Chapter 12)
Indefinite pronouns: singular and plural forms (Chapter 12)

Basic Grammar

The word for which a pronoun stands is its antecedent. Most personal and relative and some demonstrative pronouns require antecedents.

A personal pronoun takes the singular or plural form to agree with its antecedent in number.

The use of first, second, or third person forms for personal pronouns must be logical and consistent.

In the third person singular, personal pronouns agree with antecedents in gender.

Putting It to Work

1. In order to decide whether you need a singular or plural personal pronoun, you must find the antecedent and determine whether it is singular or plural. (Compare Chapter 21, "Making Verbs Agree.")

2. Use a singular pronoun to refer to a compound antecedent if it is composed of two or more singular words joined by *or* or *nor*:

WRONG: Neither Sally nor Martha will be given the leading role unless *they* improve.

RIGHT: Neither Sally nor Martha will be given the leading role unless *she* improves.

WRONG: Any Tom, Dick, or Harry can cancel *their* reservation at five minutes' notice.

RIGHT: Any Tom, Dick, or Harry can cancel *his* reservation at five minutes' notice.

3. Use singular pronouns to refer to these indefinite pronouns and adjectives: *one, anyone, everyone, anybody, everybody, nobody, each, every, either, neither*:

WRONG: Everybody should bring *their* own fishing equipment.

RIGHT: Everybody should bring *his* own fishing equipment.

WRONG: Each of the candidates will be allowed three minutes to explain *their* views.

RIGHT: Each of the candidates will be allowed three minutes to explain *his* views.

WRONG: Nobody would admit that *they* were tired.

RIGHT: Nobody would admit that *he* was tired.

WRONG: Every door and gatepost had *their* sign of welcome.

RIGHT: Every door and gatepost had *its* sign of welcome.

4. In general, use *his* rather than *his or her* to refer to both sexes; or reconstruct the sentence:

RIGHT: Every man and woman should consult his conscience before he votes.

5. Avoid the shift of person from third person *one* to second person *you*, or vice versa; but you may correctly use *he* or *his* to refer to *one*:

WRONG: After *one* has been sorting these applications for a few days, *you* know what mistakes to look for.

RIGHT: After one has been sorting these applications for a few days, *he* (or *one*) knows what mistakes to look for.

Practice in Making Pronouns Agree

Select the correct form from the choices given in parentheses. (Answers on p. 165)

1. If anyone has a legitimate reason for not attending, (*he, they*) should speak to the secretary.
2. Every member of the crew was decorated for (*his, their*) part in the rescue.
3. An experienced glass blower develops great lung power, but (*he becomes, they become*) liable to pulmonary diseases.
4. As soon as one does succeed in making a few millions, (*you, one, he*) (*has, have*) to start giving it away to charities.
5. Neither hot sunshine nor heavy rainfall will do any serious harm unless (*it continues, they continue*) for a week or more.
6. Every member of this large family had (*his, his or her, their*) special chores and responsibilities.
7. At this time the coroner or his assistant must be prepared to make (*his, their*) statement.
8. Each of these hundreds of tools had (*its, their*) own box or slot above the bench.
9. Despite the threatening weather, nobody thought to bring (*his, their*) umbrella.
10. If you really take up a hobby like this seriously, (*you, he*) must spend some money on it.

26

MAKING PRONOUNS CLEAR

Background

Pronoun antecedents (Chapter 12)
Personal, relative, and demonstrative pronouns (Chapter 12)
Adjective clauses (Chapter 19)

Basic Grammar

Personal, relative, and demonstrative pronouns often require antecedents.

Sentence ideas are sometimes confused by the use of a pronoun which does not have a clear antecedent. If the reference of a pronoun is ambiguous (having two meanings), or too general, or too vague, the sentence may lack clarity.

Putting It to Work

1. Avoid ambiguous reference. This occurs when a pronoun refers confusingly to two possible antecedents. In recasting such a sentence, don't use the awkward device of a parenthetical insert:

AMBIGUOUS: Harvey told his father that *he* was too old to play with the cub scouts.

AWKWARD: Harvey told his father that *he* (Harvey) was too old to play with the cub scouts.

CLEAR: Harvey said to his father, "I'm too old to play with the cub scouts."

CLEAR: Harvey felt that he was too old to play with the cub scouts. He discussed the matter with his father.

AMBIGUOUS: We took up the rugs in both rooms and cleaned *them* thoroughly for the party.

CLEAR: We took up the rugs and cleaned both rooms thoroughly for the party.

AMBIGUOUS: One of the girls had brought her younger sister, but *she* didn't have much fun on the trip.

CLEAR: One of the girls, who had brought her younger sister, didn't have much fun on the trip.

CLEAR: One of the girls had brought her younger sister, but the little girl didn't have much fun on the trip.

2. Avoid general reference. This occurs when a pronoun refers confusingly to a general idea which is vague to the reader:

GENERAL: He has thousands of books but never keeps them in any kind of order, *which* I find confusing.

CLEAR: He has thousands of books, but I am confused by the disorder in which he keeps them.

GENERAL: Read the directions printed on the bottle. *It* may save you from making a mistake.

CLEAR: Reading the directions on the bottle may prevent a mistake.

GENERAL: By taking the upper road you can avoid the traffic on Main Street, *which* will get you there in half the time.

CLEAR: You can get there in half the time if you take the upper road and avoid the traffic on Main Street.

3. Avoid weak reference. This occurs when an antecedent has not been definitely expressed, or when it appears only as a possessive modifier:

WEAK: Clifford's father died when *he* was twelve years old.

CLEAR: When Clifford was twelve years old, his father died.

WEAK: The children's lunches are all packed, and *they*'re ready to go.

CLEAR: The children are ready to go. Their lunches are all packed.

WEAK: Aunt Bessie has just weighed herself in the drug store, but she doesn't think *it's* right.

CLEAR: Aunt Bessie has just weighed herself in the drug store, but she doesn't think the scale is right.

4. Avoid the impersonal use of *they* and *it*, except in common idiomatic expressions: "It's beginning to rain"; "It must be about eight o'clock."

WRONG: In the Bay of Fundy they have the highest tides in the world.

RIGHT: The Bay of Fundy has the highest tides in the world.

WRONG: In today's newspaper *it* says that drug prices are coming down.

RIGHT: Today's newspaper says that drug prices are coming down.

COLLOQUIAL: *They* don't allow commercial vehicles on the new highway.

RIGHT: Commercial vehicles are not allowed on the new highway.

Practice in Providing Clear Antecedents

Recast the following sentences to make the pronoun reference clear.   (Answers on p. 165)

1. In Shakespeare's *Julius Caesar* he studies various facets of the political mind at work.
2. Emma told her mother that one of her stockings had a run in it.
3. I was listening to the baseball game that day when they interrupted to say that Ranger had hit the moon.
4. They don't collect garbage as often in the outlying sections.
5. At the gate of the city I passed a man riding on a great chestnut horse, who looked at me with suspicion.
6. On the map it shows what a vast territory Indonesia covers.
7. There are a number of minor characters in the book that I haven't time to discuss.
8. In Aberdeen during the epidemic they didn't become excited or panicky.

9. There are only six copies of the book in the library for a class of thirty, which isn't enough.
10. Having a bathtub in the house makes it very pleasant.
11. Willie enjoyed the water-skiing so much that he wants them for Christmas.
12. On most of the planes they serve meals without charge.
13. To avoid hitting the child he swerved and ran up on the sidewalk, which saved its life.
14. In the preface of the book it says that Bierce disappeared in Mexico.
15. During King John's reign he antagonized many of the great lords and barons.
16. I know the finish is badly scarred and one of the legs is weak, but they charged me only ten dollars for it.
17. Les told my brother that he wasn't eligible.
18. The waves were driven right up against the house fronts, and several of them collapsed.
19. Gloria's mother studied nursing as a girl, and now she herself is thinking of becoming one.
20. It says on the notice that the office will be closed on Veterans' Day.

27

USING THE RIGHT MODIFIERS

Background

Predicate adjectives (Chapter 8)
Adjectives: functions; comparison (Chapter 14)
Adverbs: functions; comparison (Chapter 15)

Basic Grammar

Adjectives are used to modify nouns or pronouns.
Adverbs are used to modify verbs, adjectives, or adverbs.

In the comparison of adjectives and adverbs, the comparative degree is used for two things, the superlative for three or more.

Two negative adverbs (*not, never, hardly, scarcely*) should not be used for the same negative idea. Violation of this rule is called a "double negative."

Putting It to Work

1. Use an adjective (predicate adjective) after such verbs as *be, appear, become, remain, seem, feel, smell, look, sound,* and *taste,* when the description applies to the subject:

> RIGHT: The acoustics were *excellent.*
> RIGHT: He appears *happy* over the results.
> RIGHT: The room remained *silent.*
> RIGHT: We all felt *bad* about his resignation.
> RIGHT: The sky looks very *grey.*

2. Use an adverb after a verb, including those listed in the preceding paragraph, when the description applies to the action of the verb:

RIGHT: The motor runs *badly* despite all our work.
RIGHT: He appeared *suddenly* on the balcony.
RIGHT: The climber felt *cautiously* for the tiny ledge.
RIGHT: We looked *mournfully* at the sky.

3. Distinguish carefully between *good*, which is never an adverb, and *well*, which is usually an adverb but has certain adjective uses:

WRONG: He worked very *good* for an hour or so.
RIGHT: He worked very *well* for an hour or so.

RIGHT: I feel *good* after that swim.
RIGHT: He seems quite *well* again.   (health)
RIGHT: She looks *well* in that dress.   (appearance)

4. Don't use the adjectives *sure* and *real* as adverbs:

WRONG: We *sure* gave them a beating.
RIGHT: We *surely* gave them a beating.

WRONG: He has a *real* good curve.
RIGHT: He has a *really* good curve.
RIGHT: He has a *very* good curve.

5. Use the comparative degree of adjectives and adverbs when comparing two things; the superlative degree only when comparing three or more things:

WRONG: The new car is *most* convenient for long trips, but the old one is *best* for driving around the city.
RIGHT: The new car is *more* convenient for long trips, but the old one is *better* for driving around the city.

WRONG: The two boys look very much alike, but Bert is the *tallest*.
RIGHT: The two boys look very much alike, but Bert is the *taller*.

6. Avoid the double comparative. Use either *-er* and *-est* or *more* and *most*—not both methods at once:

WRONG: She's *more prettier* than she used to be.
RIGHT: She's *prettier* than she used to be.
RIGHT: She's *more attractive* than she used to be.

7. Use *other* or *else* when comparing one person or thing with the rest of a group:

> WRONG: When Willie is feeling good, he plays better than *any-
> one* on his team.
>
> RIGHT: When Willie is feeling good, he plays better than *any-
> one else* on his team.

> WRONG: During this period the United States was stronger
> than *any country* in the world.
>
> RIGHT: During this period the United States was stronger
> than *any other country* in the world.

8. Don't use two negative adverbs (*not, never, hardly, scarcely*) with a single verb (double negative):

> WRONG: He had*n't hardly* left the room when the bomb ex-
> ploded.
>
> RIGHT: He had *hardly* left the room when the bomb exploded.

Practice in Using Modifiers Accurately

Select the correct form from the choices given in parentheses. (Answers on p. 166)

1. Lester pitched (*good, well*) for the first five innings.
2. That coin sounds (*right, rightly*) when you bounce it on the counter.
3. This is the (*happiest, most happiest*) morning I've ever known.
4. The score was still tied at the end of the half, but you could see that their team was the (*stronger, strongest*).
5. The committee (*has scarcely, hasn't scarcely*) had time to study the problem.
6. Captain Willetts has a better record than (*any, any other*) officer in his regiment.
7. I think the butter smells a little (*rancid, rancidly*).
8. Sonya arrived (*unexpected, unexpectedly*) at six o'clock in the morning.
9. Haven't you (*ever, never*) flown in a jet before?
10. The motor heats up (*bad, badly*) in this weather.
11. Those shoes look (*real, really*) smart with that costume.

12. (*Anyone, Anyone else*) would have put up a better fight than Frank did.
13. She's looking very (*good, well*) after the operation.
14. Clean out the pits (*good, well*) before you screw down the covers.
15. If I had to choose between the two, I'd say the Maugham book is the (*more, most*) interesting.
16. Things were beginning to look (*bad, badly*) for the entrapped regiment.
17. When Jason reached the camp, he (*was, wasn't*) hardly able to walk.
18. If you beat him, he simply becomes more (*stubborn, stubbornly*).
19. Your glass (*sure, surely*) holds more than mine does.
20. Carry that bag (*careful, carefully*), or the bottom will fall out.

28

USING THE RIGHT CONNECTIVES

Background

Prepositions (Chapter 16)
Conjunctions (Chapter 17)
Subordinate clauses (Chapter 19)
Subordinating conjunctions (Chapter 19)

Basic Grammar

A preposition introduces a prepositional phrase, and connects a noun or a pronoun to the word that the phrase modifies.

A coordinating conjunction connects sentence elements of the same grammatical class: nouns with nouns, adjectives with adjectives, main clauses with main clauses, etc.

A subordinating conjunction connects an adverb or noun subordinate clause with a word in the main clause.

Putting It to Work

1. Distinguish between prepositions that are closely related in appearance or meaning:

> *in* suggests location within a place.
> *into* suggests motion from one place to another
> (but *in* may be used as an adverb; *into* is always a preposition)
>> Stay *in* your room.
>> Come *into* my office.
>> Walk *in.*   (adverb)

between refers properly to two objects or people
among is used in referring to more than two
> There's been some difference of opinion *between* his parents.
> It's hard to choose *among* so many capable candidates.

beside means *alongside of*
besides means *in addition to*
> He has a cottage *beside* the lake.
> *Besides* this, he owns a house in town.

2. Use the preposition *from* rather than the conjunction *than* after *different*:

WRONG: This mower is *different than* the other mowers on the market today.

RIGHT: This mower is *different from* the other mowers on the market today. (*mowers* is the object of the preposition)

RIGHT: This mower is *more efficient than* the other mowers on the market today. (*mowers* is the subject in the elliptical clause)

WRONG: The neighborhood seems *different than* it used to be.

RIGHT: The neighborhood seems *different from* what it used to be. (the noun clause *what it used to be* is the object of the preposition)

3. Use *because of* or *owing to* rather than *due to* in a prepositional construction:

COLLOQUIAL: *Due to* illness, he was unable to make the trip.

RIGHT: *Because of* illness, he was unable to make the trip.

RIGHT: His absence was *due to* illness. (predicate adjective)

4. Avoid the use of the preposition *like* in place of the conjunction *as* or *as if*:

COLLOQUIAL: You look *like* you were worried about something.

RIGHT: You look *as if* you were worried about something.

RIGHT: You look *like* a man with a problem.

COLLOQUIAL: Spinach tastes good *like* a vegetable should.

RIGHT: Spinach tastes good *as* a vegetable should.

5. Use *because* or *since* rather than the vulgar *being as* or *being that*:

WRONG: *Being as* we had no plans, we wasted the afternoon.
RIGHT: *Because* we had no plans, we wasted the afternoon.

WRONG: *Being that* the traffic was heavy, we decided to stop at a motel overnight.
RIGHT: *Since* the traffic was heavy, we decided to stop at a motel overnight.

6. Use *that* rather than *because* in noun clause constructions after a linking verb:

AWKWARD: The reason for our decision *was because* prices were going up.
RIGHT: The reason for our decision *was that* prices were going up.   (linking verb—noun clause, predicate nominative)
RIGHT: Our decision was made because prices were going up.   (action verb—adverbial clause modifier)

7. Use a noun construction rather than the adverbial *when* or *where* after a linking verb, particularly in definitions:

AWKWARD: A touchdown *is when* a player carries the ball across the opponents' goal line.
RIGHT: A touchdown is a score made when a player carries the ball across the opponents' goal line.   (linking verb—predicate nominative)
RIGHT: A touchdown occurs when a player carries the ball across the opponents' goal line.   (action verb—adverbial clause modifier)

Practice in Using the Right Connectives

In the following sentences make whatever changes are necessary to provide clear and correct connective words.   (Answers on p. 166)

1. Stuart walks like he had something wrong with his foot.
2. The arrangement of the furniture seems different than I remember it.
3. Being as time was short, we had to go without lunch.

4. Due to circumstances beyond our control, the program has been canceled.

5. Besides the lamp was a small coffee table.

6. Our real problem was when Ruth and Kathie had to work in the same room.

7. We had eighteen dollars to spend between the four of us.

8. His sinus trouble has become worse, due to the damp weather.

9. In five minutes we were chatting like we were old friends.

10. A corduroy road is when there are parallel ridges running across it.

11. The climate here is much different than what I'm used to.

12. An additional problem was because we couldn't hammer nails into the steel walls.

13. Bring your work in the library, where it's quiet.

14. Due to the holiday weekend, we couldn't book passage on a plane.

15. We had to distribute our meagre furnishings between the living room, the dining room, and two bedrooms.

16. If you had come early like you promised, we'd be finished now.

17. Fires have been occurring rather frequently, due to carelessness on the part of campers.

18. Being that the term is practically over, I'm looking for a summer job.

19. She sang like she really enjoyed it.

20. The reason for the failure of our campaign was because we had no money for advertising.

29

MAKING SENTENCES COMPLETE AND UNIFIED

Background

Subject and predicate (Chapter 1)
Verbals (Chapter 10)
Appositives (Chapter 13)
Conjunctions (Chapter 17)
Kinds of sentences (Chapter 18)
Subordinate clauses (Chapter 19)

Basic Grammar

A sentence must be logically and grammatically complete; that is, it must contain a subject and a predicate.

A sentence must be able to stand by itself.

A sentence must end with a period, a question mark, or an exclamation point; but a semicolon may be used as a grammatical stop between main clauses.

A *fragment* is a part of a sentence punctuated as though it were a complete sentence.

A *run-on* is two sentences run together and punctuated as one.

Putting It to Work

1. Make sure that every subordinate construction you write (subordinate clause, appositive phrase, verbal phrase, etc.) is attached to a main clause in the same sentence.   Avoid fragments:

WRONG: We usually go to the fair in the evening. Because everything is more glamorous under the lights. (Main clause. Subordinate clause.)

RIGHT: We usually go to the fair in the evening, because everything is more glamorous under the lights. (Fragment included with the main clause.)

RIGHT: We usually go to the fair in the evening. Everything is more glamorous under the lights. (Fragment made into a separate sentence.)

WRONG: After all the children are tucked away peacefully in the darkened house. Mother breathes a deep sigh of relief. (Subordinate clause. Main clause.)

RIGHT: After all the children are tucked away peacefully in the darkened house, Mother breathes a deep sigh of relief. (Fragment included with the main clause.)

WRONG: He is a remarkably successful leader and a powerful political force. A man with friends in every state in the Union. (Main clause. Appositive phrase.)

RIGHT: He is a remarkably successful leader and a powerful political force, a man with friends in every state in the Union. (Fragment included with main clause.)

WRONG: We had to hang a heavy blanket before the tent opening. To keep out inquisitive woodchucks and porcupines. (Main clause. Infinitive phrase.)

RIGHT: We had to hang a heavy blanket before the tent opening to keep out inquisitive woodchucks and porcupines. (Fragment included with the main clause.)

WRONG: Having spent five years to complete his studies for the degree of B.A. Our friend decided to work for a Master's degree. Which would require at least another year of work. (Participial phrase. Main clause. Subordinate clause.)

RIGHT: Having spent five years to complete his studies for the degree of B.A., our friend decided to work for a Master's degree, which would require at least another year of work. (Both fragments included with the main clause.)

2. Make sure, if you have two main clauses in the same sentence, that you set a full-stop punctuation mark between them, or use an appropriate conjunction.   Avoid run-ons:

WRONG: The only light in the room was very dim, I couldn't read my book.

RIGHT: The only light in the room was very dim.   I couldn't read my book.   (period)

RIGHT: The only light in the room was very dim; I couldn't read my book.   (semicolon)

RIGHT: The only light in the room was very dim; consequently I couldn't read my book.   (semicolon, plus a conjunctive adverb)

RIGHT: The only light in the room was very dim, and I couldn't read my book.   (coordinating conjunction)

RIGHT: The only light in the room was so dim that I couldn't read my book.   (subordinating conjunction *so that*)

RIGHT: Because the light in the room was very dim, I couldn't read my book.   (subordinating conjunction *because*)

WRONG: The howling seemed to fade away for a moment or two, then I heard it again.

RIGHT: The howling seemed to fade away for a moment or two.   Then I heard it again.   (period)

RIGHT: The howling seemed to fade away for a moment or two; then I heard it again.   (semicolon)

RIGHT: The howling seemed to fade away for a moment or two, but then I heard it again. (coordinating conjunction)

RIGHT: Although the howling seemed to fade away for a moment or two, I soon heard it again. (subordinating conjunction)

Where, as in these sentences, you have a wide choice of alternatives, you should naturally use the one that seems clearest and most expressive.

3. Don't begin sentences with coordinating conjunctions, except in informal writing:

INFORMAL: The wind was working up into a gale.   And the rain, blown straight into our faces, was cold and piercing.

RIGHT: The wind was working up into a gale; and the rain, blown straight into our faces, was cold and piercing.

INFORMAL: Martin has a belligerent manner and a disagreeable personality. But he does his job and does it well.

RIGHT: Martin has a belligerent manner and a disagreeable personality. However, he does his job and does it well.

4. Don't be confused by a broken quotation. Note whether it is broken between sentences or between the parts of a sentence, and punctuate accordingly:

WRONG: "Haven't I seen you somewhere?" he asked, "aren't you Mae Skelly's brother?"

RIGHT: "Haven't I seen you somewhere?" he asked. "Aren't you Mae Skelly's brother?"

WRONG: "Sometimes I wonder," he said. "Why I ever hired you."

RIGHT: "Sometimes I wonder," he said, "why I ever hired you."

Practice in Writing Complete Sentences

In the following, write *S* next to each complete sentence (main clause). Make each incomplete construction into a good sentence by recasting it into a main clause or by adding a main clause to it. (Answers on p. 167)

1. Although the trousers were really too short.
2. After a few minutes the crowd dispersed quietly.
3. Why he made such a remark.
4. Why have you brought the daggers from the chamber?
5. Where there's smoke, there's fire.
6. The man who financed the campaign.
7. While you were sitting here and smoking complacently.
8. Having applied for help to everyone we could think of.
9. The air felt fresh, but the water was warm.
10. If at first you don't succeed, try again.
11. That the answers were in the back of the book.
12. There isn't any other road.

13. To make a long story short.
14. In the summer she goes to a cottage on Lake Ontario.
15. In the corner where the radio used to stand.
16. But not without a great deal of time and effort.
17. Put a little in the water when you wash.
18. Whenever it suits my purposes.
19. A man with gold-rimmed spectacles and a grey mustache.
20. That was an excellent production.

Practice in Writing Unified Sentences

In the following, write *S* next to each complete and unified sentence. Provide proper punctuation and connective words where needed. (Answers on p. 168)

1. Be sure to close all the windows, it might rain while we're away.
2. Macaulay was an outstanding liberal, although he belonged to the aristocracy.
3. Isn't there any easier way, we can't walk that distance with the children and all the suitcases.
4. He has a good mind and a wide range of interests despite his poor eyesight he has taught himself several languages.
5. "Don't bother to come to the train with me," she said, "it's only a short walk."
6. Sarah was in the middle of housecleaning when the new rug came and she had to stop everything.
7. First the house began to tremble, then with a loud crash the big picture fell from over the fireplace.
8. "Don't touch anything," he commanded, "or you'll have trouble when the police come."
9. Barbara arrived this morning for a visit, we were horrified, we hadn't expected her till next week.
10. I like tea, Kenneth likes coffee.
11. He's been out there all morning and he hasn't finished the weeding yet.
12. Every now and then we passed a tinker's cart, gaily painted and decorated with bells, but drawn by a rather bedraggled horse.
13. "Is it any wonder that you're getting thin?" she exclaimed in exasperation, "you never eat your dinner."

14. The place is rather bare and rocky, however, the climate is generally temperate and there are no flies or mosquitoes.

15. After his year in Paris his style changed, and he began to use a kind of cubist technique, with very bright colors.

16. If the play doesn't end by eleven, I'll have to leave anyway, the last train goes at twenty after.

17. Buying the film is no problem, it's the developing that costs so much.

18. Why don't you telephone, if she doesn't want to speak to you, she can hang up.

19. My watch has been losing time ever since last Sunday, when I forgot to take it off in the shower.

20. Ann is doing very well now, in fact, she makes more money than I do.

PLACING MODIFIERS CLEARLY

Background

Verbals as modifiers (Chapter 10)
Adjectives as modifiers (Chapter 14)
Adverbs as modifiers (Chapter 15)
Prepositional phrases as modifiers (Chapter 16)
Subordinate clauses as modifiers (Chapter 19)

Basic Grammar

Modifiers, whether single words or groups of words, function as either adjectives or adverbs:

as adjectives, to modify nouns or pronouns
as adverbs, to modify verbs, adjectives, or adverbs

If a modifier is a single word, a prepositional phrase, or a subordinate clause, it should be clearly attached to the word it modifies by careful placing in the sentence. A "misplaced" or "squinting" modifier may produce ambiguity.

If a modifier is an infinitive (*to go*), a participle (*going*), or a gerund governed by a preposition (*by going*), it requires special treatment. Such a word, being a verbal, has some qualities of a verb and refers to an implied subject. Failure to supply this subject in the sentence produces a "dangling" modifier.

Putting It to Work

1. Avoid ambiguity by placing word, phrase, and clause modifiers in a position where they clearly modify the right word. A problem may arise when we have two modifiers for the same word:

books *in the bag*
books *that he had bought in England*

Careless phrasing might produce this sentence:

WRONG: There were several books in the bag that he had
bought in England.

The clause modifier *that he had bought in England* is ambiguous; it
may refer to *books* or *bag*.

By rearranging the misplaced modifier, the clause can be made
to refer clearly to either word:

RIGHT: In the bag were several books that he had bought in
England.

RIGHT: In the bag that he had bought in England, there were
several books.

Similarly:

WRONG: He declined to take advantage of my offer *completely*.
RIGHT: He declined completely to take advantage of my offer.
RIGHT: He declined to take complete advantage of my offer.

WRONG: We could see smoke rising from our neighbor's
chimney *with a pair of binoculars*.
RIGHT: With a pair of binoculars we could see smoke rising
from our neighbor's chimney.

Sometimes, in the middle of a sentence, a modifier may "squint"
between two possible meanings:

WRONG: People who eat heavy meals *frequently* have stomach
trouble.
RIGHT: People who eat frequent heavy meals have stomach
trouble.
RIGHT: People who eat heavy meals have stomach trouble
frequently.

WRONG: A woman who was waving a towel *frantically* screamed
at us.
RIGHT: A woman who was waving a towel screamed at us
frantically.
RIGHT: A woman who was frantically waving a towel screamed
at us.

Sometimes a squinting modifier should really have the effect of a sentence modifier, applying to the entire idea rather than just one word.   In that case it is usually clearer at the beginning:

> WRONG: The men who died *often* had no identification.
> RIGHT: Often the men who died had no identification.

2. Avoid dangling modifiers, which are usually participles but may be any kind of verbal.   Remember that a subject is implied, and that you must include that subject word at the beginning of the main clause:

> *Seeing* Jenny at the station . . .   (participle)
> *To see* Jenny at the station . . .   (infinitive)
> *By seeing* Jenny at the station . . .   (gerund)

Someone is obviously seeing or planning to see Jenny.   Careful phrasing requires that we supply the appropriate subject at the beginning of the main clause:

> WRONG: *Seeing* Jenny at the station, the *surprise* was over-whelming.
> RIGHT: *Seeing* Jenny at the station, *we* were overwhelmed with surprise.

> WRONG: *To see* Jenny at the station, *plans* had to be made well in advance.
> WRONG: *To see* Jenny at the station, our *plans* had to be made well in advance.   (The possessive modifier *our* does not act as the subject.)
> RIGHT: *To see* Jenny at the station, *we* had to plan well in advance.

> WRONG: *By seeing* Jenny at the station, an extra *trip* was saved.
> RIGHT: *By seeing* Jenny at the station, *we* saved an extra trip.

Verbals in the passive or past participle form require the same approach:

> *Cooled* by air conditioning . . .   (participle)
> *To be cooled* by air conditioning . . .   (infinitive)
> *After being cooled* by air conditioning . . .   (gerund)

Something is cooled or to be cooled.

WRONG: *Cooled* by air conditioning, *you* could make this room
       quite comfortable.
RIGHT: *Cooled* by air conditioning, this *room* could be made
       quite comfortable.

WRONG: *To be cooled* by air conditioning, *you* would need two
       separate units for this room.
RIGHT: *To be cooled* by air conditioning, this *room* would need
       two separate units.

WRONG: *After being cooled* by air conditioning, *we* found the
       room more comfortable.
RIGHT: *After being cooled* by air conditioning, the *room* was more
       comfortable.

Recasting a dangling modifier into a subordinate clause will often
make the sentence clear:

RIGHT: When we saw Jenny at the station, the surprise was
       overwhelming.
RIGHT: If it were cooled by air conditioning, you could make
       this room quite comfortable.

Practice in Making Modifiers Clear

In the following sentences make whatever changes are necessary
to associate modifiers clearly with the words they should logically
modify.   Use your own judgment about interpretation.   (Answers
on p. 169)

1. He keeps a pipe on his desk, which he seldom uses.
2. Keep to the right of the monument of Lincoln on the way out
   of town.
3. Absorbed in a daydream, Harry's teacher spoke to him sharply.
4. That's my picture on the floor that you're stepping on.
5. Having lived most of her life in a small town, Boston was
   overwhelming.
6. Confronted with the evidence, a full confession was easily
   obtained.
7. From my desk I watched Marley like a hawk preparing for his
   interview.

8. When in Canada, Lake Louise is certainly worth seeing. (Use a subordinate clause.)
9. To finish in time for dinner, some of my homework was done rather sketchily.
10. After driving several miles on the highway, the sign showed that we were going in the wrong direction.
11. After being given three coats of shellac, you should apply a thin coat of varnish.
12. The women and children were herded into a church with scant ceremony.
13. Settling herself comfortably on the sofa, a large yellow cat jumped into her lap.
14. Seen from across the bay, one receives an impressive view of the harbor.
15. We passed several farm families in shabby wooden carts drawn by tiny donkeys on their way to the funeral.
16. The man who spoke usually has nothing to say.
17. To swim across safely, the tide should be high.
18. Bowling along at about sixty miles an hour, a jack rabbit suddenly darted out in front of the car.
19. Having paid our bills, the proprietor urged us to come again.
20. I like the doughnuts in the other case with the chocolate frosting.

31

ORGANIZING SENTENCES LOGICALLY

Background

Compound constructions (Chapter 4)
Correlative conjunctions (Chapter 17)
Kinds of sentences (Chapter 18)

Basic Grammar

In a well-constructed sentence the arrangement and phrasing should be appropriate to the meaning.

Similar (parallel) constructions should be used to emphasize the similarity of two or more thoughts in a sentence. Correlative conjunctions particularly require parallel structure.

In making two comparative statements in a sentence (*never has . . . and never will*; *as tall as . . . or taller*), either complete both statements or complete the first one and use ellipsis in the second.

Putting It to Work

1. Use parallel structure for compound elements that are similar in thought and function:

AWKWARD: We did about half the trip *by bus*, and the rest *we flew*.

RIGHT: We did about half the trip *by bus*, and the rest *by plane*.

AWKWARD: I spent my days quietly, *swimming*, *in a canoe*, and even *caught a few fish*.

RIGHT: I spent my days quietly, *swimming*, *canoeing*, and *fishing*.

RIGHT: I spent my days quietly, *swimming* and *canoeing*; I even caught a few fish. (Use a different construction if you wish to make one element distinct from the others.)

AWKWARD: *His greatest asset is* his utter reliability; *he is* weakest in experience.

RIGHT: *His greatest asset is* his utter reliability; *his worst liability is* his lack of experience.

RIGHT: *He is* completely reliable, but *he lacks* experience.

AWKWARD: Sarah wrote that *she was* homesick, and *could she* come home.

RIGHT: Sarah wrote that she *was* homesick and *would like* to come home.

RIGHT: Sarah *wrote that* she was homesick and *asked if* she could come home.

2. Make sure that the sentence elements immediately following correlative conjunctions are parallel in form:

WRONG: Each student must agree *either* to study French *or* German.

RIGHT: Each student must agree to study *either* French *or* German.

WRONG: The country is *not only* devastated by poverty *but also* by political turmoil.

RIGHT: The country is devastated *not only* by poverty *but also* by political turmoil.

RIGHT: The country is *not only* devastated by poverty, *but also* confused by political turmoil.

WRONG: She has *neither* washed the dishes *nor* did she clean the bathroom.

RIGHT: She has *neither* washed the dishes *nor* cleaned the bathroom.

3. Avoid incomplete parallelism in making a comparison:

WRONG: Our backfield is better than the other team.

RIGHT: Our backfield is better than the other team's (backfield).

WRONG: He is always torn between his love of books and his electric trains.

RIGHT: He is always torn between his love of books and his passion for his electric trains.

RIGHT: He is always torn between his books and his electric trains.

WRONG: The weather this summer is appreciably cooler than last summer.

RIGHT: The weather this summer is appreciably cooler than the weather last summer.

RIGHT: This summer's weather is appreciably cooler than last summer's.

4. Avoid the omission of necessary words in making a double statement about a subject; be sure to complete the first part:

WRONG: He is certainly as tall if not taller than his father.

RIGHT: He is certainly as tall as, if not taller than, his father.

RIGHT: He is certainly as tall as his father, if not taller.

WRONG: Mildred is one of the best, if not the best dancer at the club.

RIGHT: Mildred is one of the best dancers at the club, if not the best.

WRONG: Tokyo is as large or larger than New York.

RIGHT: Tokyo is as large as or larger than New York.

RIGHT: Tokyo is as large as New York, or larger.

WRONG: Cholmondeley never has and never will give up his British citizenship.

RIGHT: Cholmondeley never has given up his British citizenship, and never will give it up.

5. Avoid abrupt and illogical shifts in subject:

AWKWARD: A detective spent the morning at the house, but no clues were found.

RIGHT: A detective spent the morning at the house but found no clues.

AWKWARD: The picture shows a flowering tree in the foreground, and a house is in the distance.

RIGHT: The picture shows a flowering tree in the foreground and a house in the distance.

AWKWARD: Although we could not see any lightning, the
thunder could be heard clearly.

RIGHT: Although we could not see any lightning, we could
hear the thunder clearly.

Practice in Organizing Sentence Elements
(Parallel Structure)

In the following sentences use parallel structure wherever it will
help to made the ideas clearer or more logical in expression.
(Answers on p. 170)

1. The committee recommended two plans for raising money:
   selling tickets to a raffle or put on a play.
2. The postman brought three letters for Bob, and Paula got only
   one.
3. Klaus was undecided whether to refuse the money and say
   nothing or if he should go to Mr. Binstead with his information.
4. I grabbed my bag, ran down the front steps, and seeing the car
   waiting I jumped in.
5. The Palace is one of the most, if not the most expensive hotel in
   the city.
6. Lawson is a man with firm convictions and who refuses to
   compromise.
7. Students at the college often earn spending money by baby-
   sitting and some of them mow lawns.
8. The house is not only larger, but the rooms are arranged more
   conveniently.
9. We have good heat in the winter, and in summer there is air-
   conditioning.
10. I think breeding tropical fish is more interesting than stamps.
11. They had to traverse a dry, sandy plain, ford two rivers, and
    then there was a mountain range to cross.
12. The lake is eight miles long with a width of three miles.
13. Matilda never has and never will apply herself to her studies.
14. You will notice that the size of the first volume is much greater
    than the second volume.

15. Her apartment is expensively decorated, with beautiful rugs, fine old furniture, and the walls covered with original paintings.

16. From these excavations scientists have learned not only that these people were highly civilized but also brilliant artists.

17. In planing a board, study the grain of the wood, and the plane should run parallel with it.

18. Our instructor considers Faulkner as important, if not more important, than Hemingway.

19. Either turn on the heat or the window should be closed.

20. Shakespeare made extensive use of sources, like Plutarch's *Lives* for the classical period, and English history based upon Holinshed's *Chronicles*.

Part III

ANSWERS TO
PRACTICE EXERCISES

ANSWERS TO PRACTICE EXERCISES

Chapter 1

PRACTICE IN RECOGNIZING SUBJECTS AND PREDICATES (see p. 5)

1. One of the covers is missing.
2. Mrs. Wilkinson settled down comfortably in her favorite rocker.
3. Many years ago I heard the same story with a different ending.
4. New countries in Africa and the Near East have become very important in the U.N.
5. The possibility of a voyage to the moon is no longer remote.
6. Experience is the best teacher.
7. Stamped at the head of the appeal was the single word: "Refused."
8. After many years his father returned.
9. Slowly, but with increasing speed, the water began to seep through the cracks.
10. One of the most important men in the community has gone.

Chapter 2

PRACTICE IN IDENTIFYING KINDS OF SENTENCES (see p. 8)

1. *D*; 2. *Imp*; 3. *Int*; 4. *D*; 5. *D*; 6. *Imp*; 7. *Imp*; 8. *Int*; 9. *Int*; 10. *D*.

MORE PRACTICE IN RECOGNIZING SUBJECTS AND PREDICATES

1. (you) Take cover.
2. Only one of his many former followers remained loyal.

3. Which road will take me to the coast?

4. After Labor Day the rates are lowered considerably.

5. Where does your friend Stanley keep his car?

6. You will need a great many more tools for such a job.

7. (you) Arrange the cards in alphabetical order.

8. (you) Please don't bother with any of my things.

9. When does the last train for Baldwin leave today?

10. Only then did we realize the seriousness of our predicament.

Chapter 3

Practice in Finding Subject and Verb (see p. 11)
The simple subjects and verbs are as follows:

1. We cooked   2. distance added   3. dog has   4. (you) wear

5. I play   6. (you) come   7. boat pitched   8. you have

9. stories are   10. need is

More Practice in Finding Subject and Verb (see p. 12)
The subjects and verbs are as follows:

1. Two were picked

2. two-thirds were destroyed

3. I do want

4. He has been accused

5. she did decide

6. time has been

7. many would have been lost

8. We can refuse

9. (you) do expect

10. spot would be pierced

Chapter 4

Practice in Finding Compound Subjects and Predicates
(see p. 14)
The subjects and verbs are as follows:

        C   C   C
1. Men, women, children were herded

       C   C
2. music, jazz can appeal

        C   C
3. highways, roads have increased

4. we swam, sailed, fished
   (C over swam, C over sailed, C over fished)

5. (you) gather, preserve
   (C over gather, C over preserve)

6. *Hamlet, Macbeth, Othello, King Lear* are considered
   (C over Hamlet, C over Macbeth, C over Othello, C over King Lear)

7. Most have criticized, condemned
   (C over criticized, C over condemned)

8. birds, insects sang, chirped, hummed
   (C over birds, C over insects, C over sang, C over chirped, C over hummed)

9. cows, calf were
   (C over cows, C over calf)

10. you have seen, heard
    (C over seen, C over heard)

Chapter 5

PRACTICE IN FINDING COMPLEMENTS (see p. 16)
The complements are as follows:

1. ingredient   2. challenge   3. work   4. NC   5. bags, boxes
6. NC   7. medicine   8. NC   9. product   10. slice

PRACTICE IN FINDING SUBJECTS, VERBS, AND COMPLEMENTS
(see p. 17)
The subjects, verbs, and complements are as follows:

1. George has been reading NC

2. George has been reading book
   (C over book)

3. (you) do bother me
   (C over me)

4. *Queen Mary* was sailing NC

5. you have noticed change
   (C over change)

6. time is NC

7. You must give time, attention
   (C over time, C over attention)

8. city stretches NC

9. Mr. Henry is carrying flag
   (C over flag)

10. (you) take hat, coat leave house
    (C over hat, C over coat, C over house)

Chapter 6

PRACTICE IN RECOGNIZING PREPOSITIONAL PHRASES (see p. 19)
The prepositional phrases are as follows:

1. (of women's fashions)   (from year)   (to year)
2. (of candy)   (between meals)
3. (of chess)   (after dinner)
4. (On the workbench)   (of chisels)
5. (in a house)   (by the side)   (of the road)
6. (from the trawler)   (to a coastguard vessel)
7. (of the line)   (around a pole)
8. (By the end)   (of the day)
9. (of the men)   (on the project)
10. (through this door)   (by the door)   (at the other side)

Chapter 7

PRACTICE IN USING PARTS OF SPEECH (see p. 23)
Answers will vary.   The sentences below are typical:

1. *Love* thy neighbor.   (verb)
   There is no *love* between them.   (noun)
   The gold heart was a *love* token.   (adj)
2. He will not *back* the organization candidate.   (verb)
   His *back* is badly sprained.   (noun)
   Please call *back* in about an hour.   (adv)
3. You're going in the *right* direction.   (adj)
   Turn *right* at the crossroads.   (adv)
4. You'll feel better if you *fast* for twenty-four hours.   (verb)
   His *fast* was broken after three days.   (noun)
   There's a *fast* train at nine in the evening.   (adj)
   Most cars go too *fast* on this road.   (adv)
5. There were Americans present, but I didn't meet *any*.   (pro)
   Any book on this list is acceptable.   (adj)

PRACTICE IN RECOGNIZING PARTS OF SPEECH (see p. 23)

   PRO   VERB   PREP ADJ ADJ NOUN PREP NOUN
1. We must get across the Swiss border by midnight.
   VERB NOUN VERB PREP ADJ ADJ   NOUN
2. Will Carmen pay   for the broken window?

ADJ PRO PREP ADJ   NOUN   VERB   ADJ NOUN PREP ADJ
3. Every one of the students has received a letter from the
  NOUN CON ADJ NOUN
  principal or his secretary.

  ADJ   NOUN   PREP ADJ NOUN   VERB   ADV   VERB
4. The bindings of many books have been hopelessly ruined.

  ADJ   NOUN   VERB   CON ADJ PRO VERB ADJ NOUN
5. This car can be repaired, but the other is a wreck.

Chapter 8

PRACTICE IN RECOGNIZING COMPLEMENTS (see p. 27)
The complements are as follows:

1. hot, dry (*PA*)
2. danger (*DO*)
3. anyone (*IO*)   truth (*DO*)
4. *NC*
5. her (*IO*)   note (*DO*)

6. wormy (*PA*)
7. *NC*
8. twenty, ten (*DO*)
9. lieutenant (*PN*)
10. man (*IO*)   fee (*DO*)

Chapter 9

PRACTICE IN USING VERB FORMS (see p. 37)

1. frozen (*PP*)
2. flown (*PP*)
3. drank (*P*)
4. begun (*PP*)
5. taken (*PP*)
6. ran (*P*)
7. swam (*P*)
8. fallen (*PP*)
9. ridden (*PP*)
10. saw (*P*)

11. threw (*P*)
12. stolen (*PP*)
13. driven (*PP*)
14. chose (*P*)
15. knew (*P*)
16. burst (*PP*)
17. gone (*PP*)
18. did (*P*), OR has done (*PP*)
19. spoke (*P*)
20. written (*PP*)

PRACTICE IN IDENTIFYING THE PERFECT TENSES (see p. 38)
The verbs in perfect tenses are as follows:

1. have arrived (*Pr*)
2. have been complaining (*Pr*)
3. have been speaking (*Pr*)
4. has changed (*Pr*)
5. have learned (*Pr*)

6. will have satisfied (*F*)
7. had reached (*P*)
8. has shown (*Pr*)
9. had been plodding (*P*)
10. will have won (*F*)

Chapter 10

PRACTICE IN RECOGNIZING INFINITIVES (see p. 42)
The infinitive phrases are as follows:

1. to achieve success (*Adj*)
   to see your goal clearly (*N*)
2. to say anything (*Adv*)
3. to have been one of your assistants (*Adv*)
4. move this sofa (*Adv*)
5. to reject his father's help (*N*)
6. to hear from the other members (*N*)
7. fly (*Adv*)
8. to loosen this (*Adv*)
9. to go (*Adj*)
10. to tell you the truth (*Adv*)
    to quit (*Adv*)

PRACTICE IN RECOGNIZING PARTICIPLES AND GERUNDS (see p. 42)
The participial and gerund phrases are as follows:

1. Trespassing (*G*)
2. breaking into his own house (*G*)
3. trembling with fright (*P*)
4. Abandoned by everyone (*P*)
5. Training dogs (*G*)
6. Watching his chance (*P*)
7. Having given formal notice (*P*) leaving (*G*)
8. going (*G*)
9. covered with ivy (*P*)
10. Engrossed in his book (*P*)

Chapter 11

PRACTICE IN RECOGNIZING NOUNS (see p. 46)
The nouns are as follows:

1. series, shocks
2. party, summit, nightfall
3. binoculars, Camp Three, ledge, valley
4. Daphne du Maurier, book, father
5. brother, attack, flu
6. way, truth
7. ship, dock
8. practitioner, arrangement
9. fears
10. member, group, leader, deal, trouble

PRACTICE IN USING CAPITAL LETTERS (see p. 47)

1. During the summer we swam in Long Island Sound.
2. We will be staying at the Willard Parker Hotel on Monday.
3. The Northwest is the source of some of the main tributaries of the Mississippi River.

4. The camp is about a mile to the east of the river.
5. The Emancipation Proclamation was signed during the third year of the Civil War.

PRACTICE IN FORMING PLURALS AND POSSESSIVES (see p. 47)

SINGULAR	PLURAL	POSSESSIVE SINGULAR	POSSESSIVE PLURAL
1. secretary	secretaries	secretary's	secretaries'
2. child	children	child's	children's
3. woman	women	woman's	women's
4. Negro	Negroes	Negro's	Negroes'
5. boy	boys	boy's	boys'
6. son-in-law	sons-in-law	son-in-law's	sons-in-law's
7. lady	ladies	lady's	ladies'
8. church	churches	church's	churches'
9. Englishman	Englishmen	Englishman's	Englishmen's
10. fox	foxes	fox's	foxes'
11. chief	chiefs	chief's	chiefs'
12. monkey	monkeys	monkey's	monkeys'
13. mosquito	mosquitoes	mosquito's	mosquitoes'
14. alumnus	alumni	alumnus's	alumni's
15. baby	babies	baby's	babies'
16. soprano	sopranos	soprano's	sopranos'
17. wolf	wolves	wolf's	wolves'
18. deer	deer	deer's	deer's
19. attorney	attorneys	attorney's	attorneys'
20. policeman	policemen	policeman's	policemen's

Chapter 12

PRACTICE WITH PERSONAL PRONOUNS AND ADJECTIVES (see p. 55)

1. The boys complained that Myra had taken their skates.

2. No one should leave his seat without permission.

3. Each man naturally thinks of himself first.

4. Several customers accused the proprietor of cheating them.

5. If anyone wants the book, give it to him.

6. The height of the building is its chief distinction.

7. Both of the farmers succeeded in selling their hogs.

8. Everyone must have a good strong stick. He will need it in these woods.

9. Neither of those workers is worth his salt.

10. A girl can really enjoy herself at the lake.

PRACTICE IN RECOGNIZING USES OF PRONOUNS (see p. 56)

1. DO OP S OP
    Give it to them if they ask for it.
    S IO

2. S
    Who told you that story?
    S PN S

3. How did he know whose it was?
    S S

4. I don't know who took the crullers.
    OP S

5. To him that hath shall be given.
    DO S

6. The leader may choose whomever he wishes.
    S

7. The police promised leniency to whoever would confess.
    S DO S

8. She's going with the boy whom she met at the dance.
    DO S OP

9. The package that I forgot to mail was for you.
    DO S OP

10. What do you know about him?

PRACTICE IN USING INDEFINITE PRONOUNS (see p. 56)

The answers below are the most likely, but there may be other possibilities:

1. Each, Every one
2. None
3. None, All, Several
4. Anyone, Anybody
5. either, one
6. any, all
7. Some, Most
8. everyone, everybody
9. Some, All, Most
10. No one, Nobody

Chapter 13

PRACTICE IN RECOGNIZING APPOSITIVES (see p. 58)
The appositives (underlined) and the words with which they are
in apposition are as follows:

1. friend—blacksmith

2. city—Halifax   seaport—terminus

3. Dr. Loomis—member

4. weakness—lack

5. you—boys   car—station wagon

6. reply—one

7. Two—Harriet, I   thriller—*The Spy Who Came In from the Cold*

8. family—mother, father, children

9. varieties—McIntosh, Delicious

10. sister—Jean   classmate—Angus Robey

Chapter 14

PRACTICE IN IDENTIFYING ADJECTIVES (see p. 62)
The adjectives are as follows:

1. new, simpler (*PA*)
2. accurate, realistic, every
3. female, green (*PA*)
4. Stormy, whole
5. thick, wet, yellow
6. Fourteen, this, deadly
7. local, blind
8. reluctant (*PA*), newly-appointed
9. Your, overwhelming (*PA*)
10. better, hardship

PRACTICE IN DISTINGUISHING ADJECTIVES FROM PRONOUNS (see p. 62)
The adjectives and pronouns are as follows:

1. This (P), everything (P)
2. Many (P), my (A), your (A)
3. Anyone (P), who (P), several (A)
4. any (A), what (P), he (P)
5. All (A), their (A), every (A)
6. More (A), this (A), it (P)
7. little (A), our (A), another (A)
8. Which (A), they (P), their (A), new (A)
9. Each (P), you (P), something (P), that (A)
10. They (P), each other (P)

PRACTICE IN COMPARING ADJECTIVES (see p. 63)

1. tinier, tiniest
2. severer, severest
3. more adequate, most adquate
4. faster, fastest
5. generally not compared
6. generally not compared
7. darker, darkest
8. better, best
9. brainier, brainiest
10. politer, politest
11. smaller, smallest
12. more distant, most distant
13. more careful, most careful
14. more awkward, most awkward
15. narrower, narrowest
16. more distinct, most distinct
17. generally not compared
18. generally not compared
19. more timid, most timid
20. generally not compared

Chapter 15

PRACTICE IN RECOGNIZING ADVERBS (see p. 67)
The adverbs are as follows:

1. almost
2. Meanwhile, by
3. away, well
4. over, further
5. Indeed, very
6. often, around
7. never, enough
8. always
9. not, very
10. more, less

PRACTICE IN DISTINGUISHING ADVERBS, ADJECTIVES, AND PREPOSITIONS (see p. 68)

1. threatingly (Adv)
2. in (Adv)
3. sure (PA), in (P)
4. happier (PA), harder (Adv)
5. around (Adv), carefully (Adv)
6. around (P), wonderingly (Adv)
7. hard (PA), well (Adv)
8. up (Adv), early (Adv)
9. jauntily (Adv), up (P)
10. more (Adv), hopeful (PA)

Chapter 16

PRACTICE IN IDENTIFYING PREPOSITIONAL PHRASES (see p. 71)

1. Henry looked around (for the owner) *Adv* (of the shop) *Adj*.

2. We stood (on the steps) *Adv* and waited patiently (for a chance) *Adv* to look inside.

3. The children (from the neighborhood) *Adj* gazed (at us) *Adv* (in amazement) *Adv*.

4. (With one exception) *Adj* the members (of the committee) *Adj* were satisfied.

5. (Beneath his rugged exterior) *Adv* he has a heart (of gold) *Adj*.

6. (Throughout the play) *Adv* I had an impression (of impending doom) *Adj*.

7. Pamela likes to read books (about travel and adventure) *Adj*.

8. The two cars raced (through the main street) *Adv* and headed (for the open country) *Adv*.

9. The shelves were loaded (with a collection) *Adv* (of old leather volumes) *Adj* (with stained and ragged covers) *Adj*.

10. (During the night) *Adv* (in the cave) *Adj* Rudolph gained tremendous respect (for his native friends) *Adj*.

Chapter 17

PRACTICE IN RECOGNIZING COORDINATING CONJUNCTIONS (see p. 74)

The coordinating conjunctions and the parts of speech they are connecting are as follows:

1. and (adjectives)
2. or (clauses)
3. not only—but (adjectives)
4. and (prepositional phrases)
5. or (prepositional phrases)
6. but (clauses)
7. and (adverbs)
8. and (nouns)
9. yet (clauses)
10. neither—nor (verbs)

PRACTICE IN RECOGNIZING SUBORDINATING CONJUNCTIONS (see p. 75)

Only the subordinate clauses are reprinted here:

1. Unless I'm much mistaken
2. because I say so
3. until all the guests arrive
4. when the fire broke out
5. If the weather continues like this
6. After all the hunters were asleep
7. because we have more possessions
8. Though we had little strength left
9. When the bell rings
10. unless you keep still

Chapter 18

PRACTICE IN RECOGNIZING KINDS OF SENTENCES (see p. 78)

1. A slight sound behind him brought him to his feet.   (simple)
2. The idea (that you suggest) seems brilliant.   (complex)
3. He advanced to the platform (on which Bentley was standing).   (complex)
4. (When you've had such an experience), you may recover, but you'll never be the same.   (compound-complex)
5. I don't know (what I can say).   (complex)
6. By the middle of the afternoon we had given up all hope of rescue.   (simple)
7. All of his shirts looked (as if they had been slept in).   (complex)
8. Take a cup of flour and work it into the mixture (until it is thoroughly blended).   (compound-complex)
9. The grass must be mowed (before the sun is too hot).   (complex)
10. Not only have you burned my toast but you've spoiled my appetite.   (compound)

Chapter 19

PRACTICE IN IDENTIFYING ADJECTIVE AND ADVERB CLAUSES (see p. 84)

1. The evil (that men do) lives after them.

2. The only thing (we have to fear) is fear itself.   —Adj

3. (Until Mr. Kinnick arrived), nothing happened.   Adv

4. The second half of the test is easier (than the first half).   —Adv

5. She is always in a state of expectation (when the postman brings a letter).   — Adv

6. (Until he was in his fifties), Mr. Steiner lived in Austria, (where he was a famous chef).   Adv   —Adj

7. (When the drought had lasted for about three weeks), the water supply became dangerously low.   Adv

8. We were annoyed by the billboards, (which obscured most of the scenery).   — Adj

9. (Since you obviously disapprove), why don't you resign?   Adv

10. She always sends me a note (if I miss anything) (that seems important).   —Adv   —Adj

PRACTICE IN IDENTIFYING NOUN CLAUSES (see p. 84)

1. I believe (that a stronger argument could be made).   O V

2. It was known (that Honeywell was prejudiced).   S

3. Does he know (where you went)?   O V

4. According to (what he says), the polls cannot be taken seriously.   O P

5. The consensus was (that the plan should be abandoned).   P N

6. (What you're saying) is (that people change).   S   P N

7. The fact (that a statesman is also a politician) doesn't detract from his statesmanship.   Ap

8. It is true (that certain requirements must be met).   S

9. (Whoever made the statement) is misinformed.   S

10. I never worry about (what I can't help).   O P

Chapter 21

PRACTICE IN MAKING VERBS AGREE (see p. 102)

1. is	7. has	13. complete	19. have	25. provides
2. weren't	8. need	14. has	20. calls	26. isn't
3. was	9. receives	15. is	21. is	27. weren't
4. doesn't	10. has	16. were	22. Here are	28. seems
5. is	11. requires	17. has	23. was	29. blow
6. have	12. doesn't	18. is	24. There's	30. is

Chapter 22

PRACTICE IN SUPPLYING PARTS OF IRREGULAR VERBS (see p. 107)

PRESENT	PAST	P.P.	PRESENT	PAST	P.P.
1. begin	began	begun	14. freeze	froze	frozen
2. break	broke	broken	15. go	went	gone
3. bring	brought	brought	16. lay	laid	laid
4. choose	chose	chosen	17. lead	led	led
5. come	came	come	18. lie	lay	lain
6. do	did	done	19. run	ran	run
7. draw	drew	drawn	20. see	saw	seen
8. drink	drank	drunk	21. shake	shook	shaken
9. drive	drove	driven	22. sink	sank	sunk
10. eat	ate	eaten	23. swear	swore	sworn
11. fall	fell	fallen	24. tear	tore	torn
12. fly	flew	flown	25. write	wrote	written
13. forget	forgot	forgotten			

PRACTICE IN SELECTING CORRECT VERB FORMS (see p. 108)

1. broken	6. drunk	11. lay	16. take
2. lying	7. May	12. Will	17. affected
3. accept	8. saw	13. Set	18. passed
4. gone	9. laid	14. led	19. frozen
5. Shall	10. sang	15. let	20. Shall

Chapter 23

PRACTICE IN CHOOSING THE RIGHT TENSE AND MOOD (see p. 111)

1. to drive
2. had
3. were
4. decided
5. spoke
6. doesn't
7. had won
8. didn't
9. caught, had escaped, screamed

10. were
11. looked
12. to hear
13. have collected
14. wanted
15. had attacked
16. had
17. to meet

18. doesn't
19. had dispersed
20. was
21. were
22. saw
23. had cleared
24. to hear
25. had arrived

Chapter 24

PRACTICE IN DETERMINING THE CASE OF PRONOUNS (see p. 116)

1. Whom
2. he
3. Whomever
4. you
5. our

6. her
7. whom
8. me
9. me
10. we

11. she, who
12. Whose
13. whoever
14. I
15. me

16. its
17. Whom
18. who
19. his
20. who

21. she
22. It's, its
23. whoever
24. I
25. he

Chapter 25

PRACTICE IN MAKING PRONOUNS AGREE (see p. 119)

1. he
2. his
3. he becomes
4. one (OR he) has
5. it continues
6. his
7. his
8. its
9. his
10. you

Chapter 26

PRACTICE IN PROVIDING CLEAR ANTECEDENTS (see p. 122)
(There may be several correct versions.)

1. In *Julius Caesar* Shakespeare studies various facets of the political mind at work.
2. Emma said, "Mother, one of your stockings has a run in it."
3. I was listening to the baseball game that day when an announcer interrupted to say that Ranger had hit the moon.
4. Garbage isn't collected as often in the outlying sections.
5. At the gate of the city a man riding on a great chestnut horse looked at me with suspicion as I passed.
6. The map shows what a vast territory Indonesia covers.

7. In the book there are a number of minor characters that I haven't time to discuss.
8. During the epidemic the people of Aberdeen didn't become excited or panicky.
9. In the library there are only six copies of the book, which isn't enough for a class of thirty.
10. It is very pleasant to have a bathtub in the house.
11. Willie enjoyed the water-skiing so much that he wants water-skis for Christmas.
12. On most of the planes meals are served without charge.
13. To avoid hitting the child he swerved and ran up on the sidewalk, thus saving the child's life.
14. The book points out in the preface that Bierce disappeared in Mexico.
15. King John during his reign antagonized many of the great lords and barons.
16. I know the table has a weak leg and a badly scarred finish, but it cost me only ten dollars.
17. Les wasn't eligible, according to what he told my brother.
18. The waves were driven right up against the fronts of the houses, several of which collapsed.
19. Gloria's mother studied nursing as a girl, and now Gloria herself is thinking of becoming a nurse.
20. The notice states that the office will be closed on Veterans' Day.

Chapter 27

PRACTICE IN USING MODIFIERS ACCURATELY (see p. 126)

1. well	6. any other	11. really	16. bad
2. right	7. rancid	12. Anyone else	17. was
3. happiest	8. unexpectedly	13. well	18. stubborn
4. stronger	9. ever	14. well	19. surely
5. has scarcely	10. badly	15. more	20. carefully

Chapter 28

PRACTICE IN USING THE RIGHT CONNECTIVES (see p. 130)
(There may be several correct versions.)

1. Stuart walks as if he had something wrong with his foot.
2. The arrangement of the furniture seems different from what I remember.

3. Since time was short, we had to go without lunch.
4. Because of circumstances beyond our control, the program has been canceled.
5. Beside the lamp was a small coffee table.
6. Our real problem came when Ruth and Kathie had to work in the same room.
7. We had eighteen dollars to spend among the four of us.
8. His sinus trouble has become worse because of the damp weather.
9. In five minutes we were chatting like old friends.
10. A corduroy road is one with parallel ridges running across it.
11. The climate here is much different from what I'm used to.
12. An additional problem was that we couldn't hammer nails into the steel walls.
13. Bring your work into the library, where it's quiet.
14. Because of the holiday weekend we couldn't book passage on a plane.
15. We had to distribute our meagre furnishings among the living room, the dining room, and two bedrooms.
16. If you had come early as you promised, we'd be finished now.
17. Fires have been occurring rather frequently, owing to carelessness on the part of campers.
18. Since the term is practically over, I'm looking for a summer job.
19. She sang as if she really enjoyed it.
20. The reason for the failure of our campaign was that we had no money for advertising.

Chapter 29

Practice in Writing Complete Sentences (see p. 135)
(There may be many correct versions.)

1. The trousers were really too short.
2. *S*
3. Why did he make such a remark?
4. *S*
5. *S*
6. He is the man who financed the campaign.
7. While you were sitting here and smoking complacently, we washed all the dishes.

8. We applied for help to everyone we could think of.
9. *S*
10. *S*
11. We discovered that the answers were in the back of the book.
12. *S*
13. To make a long story short, we lost the game in the seventeenth inning.
14. *S*
15. We placed the lamp in the corner where the radio used to stand.
16. I finished the report, but not without a great deal of time and effort.
17. *S*
18. I attend the meetings whenever it suits my purposes.
19. A man with gold-rimmed spectacles and a grey mustache was standing in the back.
20. *S*

PRACTICE IN WRITING UNIFIED SENTENCES (see p. 136)
(There may be several correct versions.)

1. Be sure to close all the windows; it might rain while we're away.
2. *S*
3. Isn't there any easier way?   We can't walk that distance with the children and all the suitcases.
4. He has a good mind and a wide range of interests.   Despite his poor eyesight he has taught himself several languages.
5. "Don't bother to come to the train with me," she said.   "It's only a short walk."
6. *S*
7. First the house began to tremble; then with a loud crash the big picture fell from over the fireplace.
8. *S*
9. Barbara arrived this morning for a visit.   We were horrified, as we hadn't expected her till next week.
10. I like tea, but Kenneth likes coffee.
11. *S*
12. *S*
13. "Is it any wonder that you're getting thin?" she exclaimed in exasperation.   "You never eat your dinner."

14. The place is rather bare and rocky; however, the climate is generally temperate, and there are no flies or mosquitoes.
15. *S*
16. If the play doesn't end by eleven, I'll have to leave anyway, because the last train goes at twenty after.
17. Buying the film is no problem; it's the developing that costs so much.
18. Why don't you telephone? If she doesn't want to speak to you, she can hang up.
19. *S*
20. Ann is doing very well now; in fact, she makes more money than I do.

Chapter 30

PRACTICE IN MAKING MODIFIERS CLEAR (see p. 141)
(There may be many correct versions.)

1. On his desk he keeps a pipe, which he seldom uses.
2. On the way out of town keep to the right of the monument of Lincoln.
3. Because Harry was absorbed in a daydream, his teacher spoke to him sharply.
4. That's my picture that you're stepping on.
5. Having lived most of her life in a small town, she found Boston overwhelming.
6. Confronted with the evidence, he readily offered a full confession.
7. From my desk I watched Marley like a hawk, as he prepared for his interview.
8. When you are in Canada, you should certainly see Lake Louise.
9. To finish in time for dinner, I did some of my homework rather sketchily.
10. After we had driven several miles on the highway, the sign showed that we were going in the wrong direction.
11. After giving it three coats of shellac, you should apply a thin coat of varnish.
12. With scant ceremony the women and children were herded into a church.
13. As she settled herself comfortably on the sofa, a large yellow cat jumped into her lap.

14. If one looks from across the bay, one receives an impressive view of the harbor.
15. We passed several farm families on their way to the funeral, in shabby wooden carts drawn by tiny donkeys.
16. The man who spoke then usually has nothing to say.
17. To swim across safely, you should wait till the tide is high.
18. As we were bowling along at about sixty miles an hour, a jack rabbit suddenly darted out in front of the car.
19. After we had paid our bills, the proprietor urged us to come again.
20. I like the chocolate-frosted doughnuts in the other case.

Chapter 31

PRACTICE IN ORGANIZING SENTENCE ELEMENTS (PARALLEL STRUCTURE) (see p. 146)

(There may be many correct versions.)

1. The committee recommended two plans for raising money: selling tickets to a raffle or putting on a play.
2. The postman brought three letters for Bob and only one for Paula.
3. Klaus was undecided whether to refuse the money and say nothing or to go to Mr. Binstead with his information.
4. I grabbed my bag, ran down the front steps, and jumped into the waiting car.
5. The Palace is one of the most expensive hotels in the city, if not the most expensive.
6. Lawson is a man with firm convictions—a man who refuses to compromise.
7. Students at the college often earn spending money by baby-sitting or mowing lawns.
8. The house is not only larger but more convenient in the arrangement of rooms.
9. We have good heat in the winter and air-conditioning in the summer.
10. I think breeding tropical fish is more interesting than collecting stamps.
11. They had to traverse a dry, sandy plain, ford two rivers, and cross a mountain range.
12. The lake is eight miles long and three miles wide.

13. Matilda never has applied herself to her studies, and never will.
14. You will notice that the first volume is much larger than the second.
15. Her apartment is expensively decorated, with beautiful rugs, fine old furniture, and original paintings.
16. From these excavations scientists have learned that these were not only highly civilized people but brilliant artists.
17. In planing a board, study the grain of the wood and keep the plane parallel with it.
18. Our instructor considers Faulkner as important as Hemingway, if not more so.
19. Either turn on the heat or close the window.
20. Shakespeare made extensive use of sources, like Plutarch's *Lives* for the classical period and Holinshed's *Chronicles* for English history.

INDEX

Many of the items listed in this Index are explained and defined in Chapter 20, "A Dictionary of Grammatical Terms," pages 86–96.

objects
  direct 25, 26
  indirect 26, 27
omission of necessary words 145
organization of sentences 143–147
  practice exercise 146, 147
other, else in comparisons 126

parallel structure 143–147
  practice exercise 146, 147
parenthetical expressions 115
participles 41, 104, 105
  as modifiers 138, 140, 141
  dangling 138–142
  in phrases 41
  practice exercises 42, 141, 142
parts of speech 21–23
  practice exercises 23
passed, past 106
passive voice 35, 36
past perfect tense 35
past tense 33
person
  in pronouns 49
  in verbs 32
  shift in 118, 119
personal pronouns 49–51, 113–116
  case of 113–116
  compound 50, 51
phrases: *See* prepositional phrases
place, clauses of 81
plurals of nouns 44, 45
  practice exercise 47
possessive case
  adjectives in 50, 60
  forms of personal pronouns and
    adjectives 115
  nouns in 45, 46
  pronouns in 50
  with gerund 114, 115
  practice exercise 47
predicate adjectives 26, 59, 124
predicate complements 25
predicate nominatives 25
predicates and subjects 3, 4, 7, 8
prepositional phrases 18–20, 69, 70, 99
  practice exercises 19, 20, 71

prepositions 18, 69–71
  at end of sentence 70
  list of 69
  practice exercise 71
  See also connectives
present perfect tense 35
present tense 33
principal parts of verbs 28–30
progressive forms of verbs 32, 33
pronouns
  agreement 117–119
  antecedents of 48, 117–123
  avoiding emphatic form 115
  case of 49, 50, 113–116
  clear reference of 120–123
  gender of 49
  impersonal *it* 50
  kinds of 49–55
    compound personal 50
    demonstrative 53
    indefinite 54
    indefinite relative 52
    interrogative 52, 53, 115
    personal 49–51
    reciprocal 55
    relative 51, 52, 115
  number of 49
  practice exercises 55, 56, 116, 119, 122, 123
proper nouns 43, 44
punctuation of run-on sentences
  See run-ons
purpose, clauses of 81

quotations, broken 135

real used incorrectly 125
reciprocal pronouns 55
reference of pronouns 120–123
  practice exercise 122, 123
relative adjectives 60
relative clauses 79, 101, 115
relative pronouns 51, 52, 115
  indefinite 52
restrictive appositives 58
result, clauses of 81
run-ons 132–137
  practice exercise 136, 137

A CATALOG OF SELECTED
DOVER BOOKS
IN ALL FIELDS OF INTEREST

A CATALOG OF SELECTED DOVER
BOOKS IN ALL FIELDS OF INTEREST

CONCERNING THE SPIRITUAL IN ART, Wassily Kandinsky. Pioneering work by father of abstract art. Thoughts on color theory, nature of art. Analysis of earlier masters. 12 illustrations. 80pp. of text. 5⅜ x 8½. 23411-8 Pa. $3.95

ANIMALS: 1,419 Copyright-Free Illustrations of Mammals, Birds, Fish, Insects, etc., Jim Harter (ed.). Clear wood engravings present, in extremely lifelike poses, over 1,000 species of animals. One of the most extensive pictorial sourcebooks of its kind. Captions. Index. 284pp. 9 x 12. 23766-4 Pa. $12.95

CELTIC ART: The Methods of Construction, George Bain. Simple geometric techniques for making Celtic interlacements, spirals, Kells-type initials, animals, humans, etc. Over 500 illustrations. 160pp. 9 x 12. (USO) 22923-8 Pa. $9.95

AN ATLAS OF ANATOMY FOR ARTISTS, Fritz Schider. Most thorough reference work on art anatomy in the world. Hundreds of illustrations, including selections from works by Vesalius, Leonardo, Goya, Ingres, Michelangelo, others. 593 illustrations. 192pp. 7⅛ x 10¼. 20241-0 Pa. $9.95

CELTIC HAND STROKE-BY-STROKE (Irish Half-Uncial from "The Book of Kells"): An Arthur Baker Calligraphy Manual, Arthur Baker. Complete guide to creating each letter of the alphabet in distinctive Celtic manner. Covers hand position, strokes, pens, inks, paper, more. Illustrated. 48pp. 8¼ x 11. 24336-2 Pa. $3.95

EASY ORIGAMI, John Montroll. Charming collection of 32 projects (hat, cup, pelican, piano, swan, many more) specially designed for the novice origami hobbyist. Clearly illustrated easy-to-follow instructions insure that even beginning papercrafters will achieve successful results. 48pp. 8¼ x 11. 27298-2 Pa. $3.50

THE COMPLETE BOOK OF BIRDHOUSE CONSTRUCTION FOR WOODWORKERS, Scott D. Campbell. Detailed instructions, illustrations, tables. Also data on bird habitat and instinct patterns. Bibliography. 3 tables. 63 illustrations in 15 figures. 48pp. 5¼ x 8½. 24407-5 Pa. $2.50

BLOOMINGDALE'S ILLUSTRATED 1886 CATALOG: Fashions, Dry Goods and Housewares, Bloomingdale Brothers. Famed merchants' extremely rare catalog depicting about 1,700 products: clothing, housewares, firearms, dry goods, jewelry, more. Invaluable for dating, identifying vintage items. Also, copyright-free graphics for artists, designers. Co-published with Henry Ford Museum & Greenfield Village. 160pp. 8¼ x 11. 25780-0 Pa. $10.95

HISTORIC COSTUME IN PICTURES, Braun & Schneider. Over 1,450 costumed figures in clearly detailed engravings–from dawn of civilization to end of 19th century. Captions. Many folk costumes. 256pp. 8⅜ x 11¾. 23150-X Pa. $12.95

CATALOG OF DOVER BOOKS

STICKLEY CRAFTSMAN FURNITURE CATALOGS, Gustav Stickley and L. & J. G. Stickley. Beautiful, functional furniture in two authentic catalogs from 1910. 594 illustrations, including 277 photos, show settles, rockers, armchairs, reclining chairs, bookcases, desks, tables. 183pp. 6½ x 9¼. 23838-5 Pa. $9.95

AMERICAN LOCOMOTIVES IN HISTORIC PHOTOGRAPHS: 1858 to 1949, Ron Ziel (ed.). A rare collection of 126 meticulously detailed official photographs, called "builder portraits," of American locomotives that majestically chronicle the rise of steam locomotive power in America. Introduction. Detailed captions. xi + 129pp. 9 x 12. 27393-8 Pa. $12.95

AMERICA'S LIGHTHOUSES: An Illustrated History, Francis Ross Holland, Jr. Delightfully written, profusely illustrated fact-filled survey of over 200 American lighthouses since 1716. History, anecdotes, technological advances, more. 240pp. 8 x 10¾. 25576-X Pa. $12.95

TOWARDS A NEW ARCHITECTURE, Le Corbusier. Pioneering manifesto by founder of "International School." Technical and aesthetic theories, views of industry, economics, relation of form to function, "mass-production split" and much more. Profusely illustrated. 320pp. 6⅛ x 9¼. (USO) 25023-7 Pa. $9.95

HOW THE OTHER HALF LIVES, Jacob Riis. Famous journalistic record, exposing poverty and degradation of New York slums around 1900, by major social reformer. 100 striking and influential photographs. 233pp. 10 x 7⅞. 22012-5 Pa. $10.95

FRUIT KEY AND TWIG KEY TO TREES AND SHRUBS, William M. Harlow. One of the handiest and most widely used identification aids. Fruit key covers 120 deciduous and evergreen species; twig key 160 deciduous species. Easily used. Over 300 photographs. 126pp. 5⅜ x 8½. 20511-8 Pa. $3.95

COMMON BIRD SONGS, Dr. Donald J. Borror. Songs of 60 most common U.S. birds: robins, sparrows, cardinals, bluejays, finches, more—arranged in order of increasing complexity. Up to 9 variations of songs of each species. Cassette and manual 99911-4 $8.95

ORCHIDS AS HOUSE PLANTS, Rebecca Tyson Northen. Grow cattleyas and many other kinds of orchids—in a window, in a case, or under artificial light. 63 illustrations. 148pp. 5⅜ x 8½. 23261-1 Pa. $4.95

MONSTER MAZES, Dave Phillips. Masterful mazes at four levels of difficulty. Avoid deadly perils and evil creatures to find magical treasures. Solutions for all 32 exciting illustrated puzzles. 48pp. 8¼ x 11. 26005-4 Pa. $2.95

MOZART'S DON GIOVANNI (DOVER OPERA LIBRETTO SERIES), Wolfgang Amadeus Mozart. Introduced and translated by Ellen H. Bleiler. Standard Italian libretto, with complete English translation. Convenient and thoroughly portable—an ideal companion for reading along with a recording or the performance itself. Introduction. List of characters. Plot summary. 121pp. 5¼ x 8½. 24944-1 Pa. $2.95

TECHNICAL MANUAL AND DICTIONARY OF CLASSICAL BALLET, Gail Grant. Defines, explains, comments on steps, movements, poses and concepts. 15-page pictorial section. Basic book for student, viewer. 127pp. 5⅜ x 8½. 21843-0 Pa. $4.95

BRASS INSTRUMENTS: Their History and Development, Anthony Baines. Authoritative, updated survey of the evolution of trumpets, trombones, bugles, cornets, French horns, tubas and other brass wind instruments. Over 140 illustrations and 48 music examples. Corrected and updated by author. New preface. Bibliography. 320pp. 5⅜ x 8½. 27574-4 Pa. $9.95

HOLLYWOOD GLAMOR PORTRAITS, John Kobal (ed.). 145 photos from 1926-49. Harlow, Gable, Bogart, Bacall; 94 stars in all. Full background on photographers, technical aspects. 160pp. 8⅜ x 11¼. 23352-9 Pa. $12.95

MAX AND MORITZ, Wilhelm Busch. Great humor classic in both German and English. Also 10 other works: "Cat and Mouse," "Plisch and Plumm," etc. 216pp. 5⅜ x 8½. 20181-3 Pa. $6.95

THE RAVEN AND OTHER FAVORITE POEMS, Edgar Allan Poe. Over 40 of the author's most memorable poems: "The Bells," "Ulalume," "Israfel," "To Helen," "The Conqueror Worm," "Eldorado," "Annabel Lee," many more. Alphabetic lists of titles and first lines. 64pp. 5 3/16 x 8¼. 26685-0 Pa. $1.00

PERSONAL MEMOIRS OF U. S. GRANT, Ulysses Simpson Grant. Intelligent, deeply moving firsthand account of Civil War campaigns, considered by many the finest military memoirs ever written. Includes letters, historic photographs, maps and more. 528pp. 6⅛ x 9¼. 28587-1 Pa. $11.95

AMULETS AND SUPERSTITIONS, E. A. Wallis Budge. Comprehensive discourse on origin, powers of amulets in many ancient cultures: Arab, Persian Babylonian, Assyrian, Egyptian, Gnostic, Hebrew, Phoenician, Syriac, etc. Covers cross, swastika, crucifix, seals, rings, stones, etc. 584pp. 5⅜ x 8½. 23573-4 Pa. $12.95

RUSSIAN STORIES/PYCCKNE PACCKA3bl: A Dual-Language Book, edited by Gleb Struve. Twelve tales by such masters as Chekhov, Tolstoy, Dostoevsky, Pushkin, others. Excellent word-for-word English translations on facing pages, plus teaching and study aids, Russian/English vocabulary, biographical/critical introductions, more. 416pp. 5⅜ x 8½. 26244-8 Pa. $8.95

PHILADELPHIA THEN AND NOW: 60 Sites Photographed in the Past and Present, Kenneth Finkel and Susan Oyama. Rare photographs of City Hall, Logan Square, Independence Hall, Betsy Ross House, other landmarks juxtaposed with contemporary views. Captures changing face of historic city. Introduction. Captions. 128pp. 8¼ x 11. 25790-8 Pa. $9.95

AIA ARCHITECTURAL GUIDE TO NASSAU AND SUFFOLK COUNTIES, LONG ISLAND, The American Institute of Architects, Long Island Chapter, and the Society for the Preservation of Long Island Antiquities. Comprehensive, well-researched and generously illustrated volume brings to life over three centuries of Long Island's great architectural heritage. More than 240 photographs with authoritative, extensively detailed captions. 176pp. 8¼ x 11. 26946-9 Pa. $14.95

NORTH AMERICAN INDIAN LIFE: Customs and Traditions of 23 Tribes, Elsie Clews Parsons (ed.). 27 fictionalized essays by noted anthropologists examine religion, customs, government, additional facets of life among the Winnebago, Crow, Zuni, Eskimo, other tribes. 480pp. 6⅛ x 9¼. 27377-6 Pa. $10.95

FRANK LLOYD WRIGHT'S HOLLYHOCK HOUSE, Donald Hoffmann. Lavishly illustrated, carefully documented study of one of Wright's most controversial residential designs. Over 120 photographs, floor plans, elevations, etc. Detailed perceptive text by noted Wright scholar. Index. 128pp. 9¼ x 10¾. 27133-1 Pa. $11.95

THE MALE AND FEMALE FIGURE IN MOTION: 60 Classic Photographic Sequences, Eadweard Muybridge. 60 true-action photographs of men and women walking, running, climbing, bending, turning, etc., reproduced from rare 19th-century masterpiece. vi + 121pp. 9 x 12. 24745-7 Pa. $10.95

1001 QUESTIONS ANSWERED ABOUT THE SEASHORE, N. J. Berrill and Jacquelyn Berrill. Queries answered about dolphins, sea snails, sponges, starfish, fishes, shore birds, many others. Covers appearance, breeding, growth, feeding, much more. 305pp. 5¼ x 8¼. 23366-9 Pa. $8.95

GUIDE TO OWL WATCHING IN NORTH AMERICA, Donald S. Heintzelman. Superb guide offers complete data and descriptions of 19 species: barn owl, screech owl, snowy owl, many more. Expert coverage of owl-watching equipment, conservation, migrations and invasions, etc. Guide to observing sites. 84 illustrations. xiii + 193pp. 5⅜ x 8½. 27344-X Pa. $8.95

MEDICINAL AND OTHER USES OF NORTH AMERICAN PLANTS: A Historical Survey with Special Reference to the Eastern Indian Tribes, Charlotte Erichsen-Brown. Chronological historical citations document 500 years of usage of plants, trees, shrubs native to eastern Canada, northeastern U.S. Also complete identifying information. 343 illustrations. 544pp. 6½ x 9¼. 25951-X Pa. $12.95

STORYBOOK MAZES, Dave Phillips. 23 stories and mazes on two-page spreads: Wizard of Oz, Treasure Island, Robin Hood, etc. Solutions. 64pp. 8¼ x 11. 23628-5 Pa. $2.95

NEGRO FOLK MUSIC, U.S.A., Harold Courlander. Noted folklorist's scholarly yet readable analysis of rich and varied musical tradition. Includes authentic versions of over 40 folk songs. Valuable bibliography and discography. xi + 324pp. 5⅜ x 8½. 27350-4 Pa. $9.95

MOVIE-STAR PORTRAITS OF THE FORTIES, John Kobal (ed.). 163 glamor, studio photos of 106 stars of the 1940s: Rita Hayworth, Ava Gardner, Marlon Brando, Clark Gable, many more. 176pp. 8⅜ x 11¼. 23546-7 Pa. $12.95

BENCHLEY LOST AND FOUND, Robert Benchley. Finest humor from early 30s, about pet peeves, child psychologists, post office and others. Mostly unavailable elsewhere. 73 illustrations by Peter Arno and others. 183pp. 5⅜ x 8½. 22410-4 Pa. $6.95

YEKL and THE IMPORTED BRIDEGROOM AND OTHER STORIES OF YIDDISH NEW YORK, Abraham Cahan. Film Hester Street based on Yekl (1896). Novel, other stories among first about Jewish immigrants on N.Y.'s East Side. 240pp. 5⅜ x 8½. 22427-9 Pa. $6.95

SELECTED POEMS, Walt Whitman. Generous sampling from *Leaves of Grass*. Twenty-four poems include "I Hear America Singing," "Song of the Open Road," "I Sing the Body Electric," "When Lilacs Last in the Dooryard Bloom'd," "O Captain! My Captain!"—all reprinted from an authoritative edition. Lists of titles and first lines. 128pp. 5³⁄₁₆ x 8¼. 26878-0 Pa. $1.00

THE BEST TALES OF HOFFMANN, E. T. A. Hoffmann. 10 of Hoffmann's most important stories: "Nutcracker and the King of Mice," "The Golden Flowerpot," etc. 458pp. 5⅜ x 8½. 21793-0 Pa. $9.95

FROM FETISH TO GOD IN ANCIENT EGYPT, E. A. Wallis Budge. Rich detailed survey of Egyptian conception of "God" and gods, magic, cult of animals, Osiris, more. Also, superb English translations of hymns and legends. 240 illustrations. 545pp. 5⅜ x 8½. 25803-3 Pa. $13.95

FRENCH STORIES/CONTES FRANÇAIS: A Dual-Language Book, Wallace Fowlie. Ten stories by French masters, Voltaire to Camus: "Micromegas" by Voltaire; "The Atheist's Mass" by Balzac; "Minuet" by de Maupassant; "The Guest" by Camus, six more. Excellent English translations on facing pages. Also French-English vocabulary list, exercises, more. 352pp. 5⅜ x 8½. 26443-2 Pa. $8.95

CHICAGO AT THE TURN OF THE CENTURY IN PHOTOGRAPHS: 122 Historic Views from the Collections of the Chicago Historical Society, Larry A. Viskochil. Rare large-format prints offer detailed views of City Hall, State Street, the Loop, Hull House, Union Station, many other landmarks, circa 1904-1913. Introduction. Captions. Maps. 144pp. 9⅜ x 12¼. 24656-6 Pa. $12.95

OLD BROOKLYN IN EARLY PHOTOGRAPHS, 1865-1929, William Lee Younger. Luna Park, Gravesend race track, construction of Grand Army Plaza, moving of Hotel Brighton, etc. 157 previously unpublished photographs. 165pp. 8⅞ x 11¾. 23587-4 Pa. $13.95

THE MYTHS OF THE NORTH AMERICAN INDIANS, Lewis Spence. Rich anthology of the myths and legends of the Algonquins, Iroquois, Pawnees and Sioux, prefaced by an extensive historical and ethnological commentary. 36 illustrations. 480pp. 5⅜ x 8½. 25967-6 Pa. $8.95

AN ENCYCLOPEDIA OF BATTLES: Accounts of Over 1,560 Battles from 1479 B.C. to the Present, David Eggenberger. Essential details of every major battle in recorded history from the first battle of Megiddo in 1479 B.C. to Grenada in 1984. List of Battle Maps. New Appendix covering the years 1967-1984. Index. 99 illustrations. 544pp. 6½ x 9¼. 24913-1 Pa. $14.95

SAILING ALONE AROUND THE WORLD, Captain Joshua Slocum. First man to sail around the world, alone, in small boat. One of great feats of seamanship told in delightful manner. 67 illustrations. 294pp. 5⅜ x 8½. 20326-3 Pa. $5.95

ANARCHISM AND OTHER ESSAYS, Emma Goldman. Powerful, penetrating, prophetic essays on direct action, role of minorities, prison reform, puritan hypocrisy, violence, etc. 271pp. 5⅜ x 8½. 22484-8 Pa. $6.95

MYTHS OF THE HINDUS AND BUDDHISTS, Ananda K. Coomaraswamy and Sister Nivedita. Great stories of the epics; deeds of Krishna, Shiva, taken from puranas, Vedas, folk tales; etc. 32 illustrations. 400pp. 5⅜ x 8½. 21759-0 Pa. $10.95

BEYOND PSYCHOLOGY, Otto Rank. Fear of death, desire of immortality, nature of sexuality, social organization, creativity, according to Rankian system. 291pp. 5⅜ x 8½. 20485-5 Pa. $8.95

A THEOLOGICO-POLITICAL TREATISE, Benedict Spinoza. Also contains unfinished Political Treatise. Great classic on religious liberty, theory of government on common consent. R. Elwes translation. Total of 421pp. 5⅜ x 8½. 20249-6 Pa. $9.95

MY BONDAGE AND MY FREEDOM, Frederick Douglass. Born a slave, Douglass became outspoken force in antislavery movement. The best of Douglass' autobiographies. Graphic description of slave life. 464pp. 5⅜ x 8½. 22457-0 Pa. $8.95

FOLLOWING THE EQUATOR: A Journey Around the World, Mark Twain. Fascinating humorous account of 1897 voyage to Hawaii, Australia, India, New Zealand, etc. Ironic, bemused reports on peoples, customs, climate, flora and fauna, politics, much more. 197 illustrations. 720pp. 5⅜ x 8½. 26113-1 Pa. $15.95

THE PEOPLE CALLED SHAKERS, Edward D. Andrews. Definitive study of Shakers: origins, beliefs, practices, dances, social organization, furniture and crafts, etc. 33 illustrations. 351pp. 5⅜ x 8½. 21081-2 Pa. $8.95

THE MYTHS OF GREECE AND ROME, H. A. Guerber. A classic of mythology, generously illustrated, long prized for its simple, graphic, accurate retelling of the principal myths of Greece and Rome, and for its commentary on their origins and significance. With 64 illustrations by Michelangelo, Raphael, Titian, Rubens, Canova, Bernini and others. 480pp. 5⅜ x 8½. 27584-1 Pa. $9.95

PSYCHOLOGY OF MUSIC, Carl E. Seashore. Classic work discusses music as a medium from psychological viewpoint. Clear treatment of physical acoustics, auditory apparatus, sound perception, development of musical skills, nature of musical feeling, host of other topics. 88 figures. 408pp. 5⅜ x 8½. 21851-1 Pa. $10.95

THE PHILOSOPHY OF HISTORY, Georg W. Hegel. Great classic of Western thought develops concept that history is not chance but rational process, the evolution of freedom. 457pp. 5⅜ x 8½. 20112-0 Pa. $9.95

THE BOOK OF TEA, Kakuzo Okakura. Minor classic of the Orient: entertaining, charming explanation, interpretation of traditional Japanese culture in terms of tea ceremony. 94pp. 5⅜ x 8½. 20070-1 Pa. $3.95

LIFE IN ANCIENT EGYPT, Adolf Erman. Fullest, most thorough, detailed older account with much not in more recent books, domestic life, religion, magic, medicine, commerce, much more. Many illustrations reproduce tomb paintings, carvings, hieroglyphs, etc. 597pp. 5⅜ x 8½. 22632-8 Pa. $11.95

SUNDIALS, Their Theory and Construction, Albert Waugh. Far and away the best, most thorough coverage of ideas, mathematics concerned, types, construction, adjusting anywhere. Simple, nontechnical treatment allows even children to build several of these dials. Over 100 illustrations. 230pp. 5⅜ x 8½. 22947-5 Pa. $7.95

DYNAMICS OF FLUIDS IN POROUS MEDIA, Jacob Bear. For advanced students of ground water hydrology, soil mechanics and physics, drainage and irrigation engineering, and more. 335 illustrations. Exercises, with answers. 784pp. 6⅛ x 9¼. 65675-6 Pa. $19.95

SONGS OF EXPERIENCE: Facsimile Reproduction with 26 Plates in Full Color, William Blake. 26 full-color plates from a rare 1826 edition. Includes "The Tyger," "London," "Holy Thursday," and other poems. Printed text of poems. 48pp. 5¼ x 7. 24636-1 Pa. $4.95

OLD-TIME VIGNETTES IN FULL COLOR, Carol Belanger Grafton (ed.). Over 390 charming, often sentimental illustrations, selected from archives of Victorian graphics—pretty women posing, children playing, food, flowers, kittens and puppies, smiling cherubs, birds and butterflies, much more. All copyright-free. 48pp. 9¼ x 12¼. 27269-9 Pa. $7.95

PERSPECTIVE FOR ARTISTS, Rex Vicat Cole. Depth, perspective of sky and sea, shadows, much more, not usually covered. 391 diagrams, 81 reproductions of drawings and paintings. 279pp. 5⅜ x 8½. 22487-2 Pa. $7.95

DRAWING THE LIVING FIGURE, Joseph Sheppard. Innovative approach to artistic anatomy focuses on specifics of surface anatomy, rather than muscles and bones. Over 170 drawings of live models in front, back and side views, and in widely varying poses. Accompanying diagrams. 177 illustrations. Introduction. Index. 144pp. 8⅜ x11¼. 26723-7 Pa. $8.95

GOTHIC AND OLD ENGLISH ALPHABETS: 100 Complete Fonts, Dan X. Solo. Add power, elegance to posters, signs, other graphics with 100 stunning copyright-free alphabets: Blackstone, Dolbey, Germania, 97 more–including many lower-case, numerals, punctuation marks. 104pp. 8⅛ x 11. 24695-7 Pa. $8.95

HOW TO DO BEADWORK, Mary White. Fundamental book on craft from simple projects to five-bead chains and woven works. 106 illustrations. 142pp. 5⅜ x 8. 20697-1 Pa. $4.95

THE BOOK OF WOOD CARVING, Charles Marshall Sayers. Finest book for beginners discusses fundamentals and offers 34 designs. "Absolutely first rate . . . well thought out and well executed."–E. J. Tangerman. 118pp. 7¾ x 10⅝. 23654-4 Pa. $6.95

ILLUSTRATED CATALOG OF CIVIL WAR MILITARY GOODS: Union Army Weapons, Insignia, Uniform Accessories, and Other Equipment, Schuyler, Hartley, and Graham. Rare, profusely illustrated 1846 catalog includes Union Army uniform and dress regulations, arms and ammunition, coats, insignia, flags, swords, rifles, etc. 226 illustrations. 160pp. 9 x 12. 24939-5 Pa. $10.95

WOMEN'S FASHIONS OF THE EARLY 1900s: An Unabridged Republication of "New York Fashions, 1909," National Cloak & Suit Co. Rare catalog of mail-order fashions documents women's and children's clothing styles shortly after the turn of the century. Captions offer full descriptions, prices. Invaluable resource for fashion, costume historians. Approximately 725 illustrations. 128pp. 8⅜ x 11¼. 27276-1 Pa. $11.95

THE 1912 AND 1915 GUSTAV STICKLEY FURNITURE CATALOGS, Gustav Stickley. With over 200 detailed illustrations and descriptions, these two catalogs are essential reading and reference materials and identification guides for Stickley furniture. Captions cite materials, dimensions and prices. 112pp. 6½ x 9¼. 26676-1 Pa. $9.95

EARLY AMERICAN LOCOMOTIVES, John H. White, Jr. Finest locomotive engravings from early 19th century: historical (1804–74), main-line (after 1870), special, foreign, etc. 147 plates. 142pp. 11⅜ x 8¼. 22772-3 Pa. $10.95

THE TALL SHIPS OF TODAY IN PHOTOGRAPHS, Frank O. Braynard. Lavishly illustrated tribute to nearly 100 majestic contemporary sailing vessels: Amerigo Vespucci, Clearwater, Constitution, Eagle, Mayflower, Sea Cloud, Victory, many more. Authoritative captions provide statistics, background on each ship. 190 black-and-white photographs and illustrations. Introduction. 128pp. 8⅞ x 11¾. 27163-3 Pa. $13.95

EARLY NINETEENTH-CENTURY CRAFTS AND TRADES, Peter Stockham (ed.). Extremely rare 1807 volume describes to youngsters the crafts and trades of the day: brickmaker, weaver, dressmaker, bookbinder, ropemaker, saddler, many more. Quaint prose, charming illustrations for each craft. 20 black-and-white line illustrations. 192pp. 4⅝ x 6.
27293-1 Pa. $4.95

VICTORIAN FASHIONS AND COSTUMES FROM HARPER'S BAZAR, 1867–1898, Stella Blum (ed.). Day costumes, evening wear, sports clothes, shoes, hats, other accessories in over 1,000 detailed engravings. 320pp. 9⅜ x 12¼.
22990-4 Pa. $14.95

GUSTAV STICKLEY, THE CRAFTSMAN, Mary Ann Smith. Superb study surveys broad scope of Stickley's achievement, especially in architecture. Design philosophy, rise and fall of the Craftsman empire, descriptions and floor plans for many Craftsman houses, more. 86 black-and-white halftones. 31 line illustrations. Introduction 208pp. 6½ x 9¼.
27210-9 Pa. $9.95

THE LONG ISLAND RAIL ROAD IN EARLY PHOTOGRAPHS, Ron Ziel. Over 220 rare photos, informative text document origin (1844) and development of rail service on Long Island. Vintage views of early trains, locomotives, stations, passengers, crews, much more. Captions. 8⅞ x 11¾.
26301-0 Pa. $13.95

THE BOOK OF OLD SHIPS: From Egyptian Galleys to Clipper Ships, Henry B. Culver. Superb, authoritative history of sailing vessels, with 80 magnificent line illustrations. Galley, bark, caravel, longship, whaler, many more. Detailed, informative text on each vessel by noted naval historian. Introduction. 256pp. 5⅜ x 8½.
27332-6 Pa. $7.95

TEN BOOKS ON ARCHITECTURE, Vitruvius. The most important book ever written on architecture. Early Roman aesthetics, technology, classical orders, site selection, all other aspects. Morgan translation. 331pp. 5⅜ x 8½. 20645-9 Pa. $8.95

THE HUMAN FIGURE IN MOTION, Eadweard Muybridge. More than 4,500 stopped-action photos, in action series, showing undraped men, women, children jumping, lying down, throwing, sitting, wrestling, carrying, etc. 390pp. 7⅞ x 10⅝.
20204-6 Clothbd. $25.95

TREES OF THE EASTERN AND CENTRAL UNITED STATES AND CANADA, William M. Harlow. Best one-volume guide to 140 trees. Full descriptions, woodlore, range, etc. Over 600 illustrations. Handy size. 288pp. 4½ x 6⅜.
20395-6 Pa. $6.95

SONGS OF WESTERN BIRDS, Dr. Donald J. Borror. Complete song and call repertoire of 60 western species, including flycatchers, juncoes, cactus wrens, many more–includes fully illustrated booklet. Cassette and manual 99913-0 $8.95

GROWING AND USING HERBS AND SPICES, Milo Miloradovich. Versatile handbook provides all the information needed for cultivation and use of all the herbs and spices available in North America. 4 illustrations. Index. Glossary. 236pp. 5⅜ x 8½.
25058-X Pa. $6.95

BIG BOOK OF MAZES AND LABYRINTHS, Walter Shepherd. 50 mazes and labyrinths in all–classical, solid, ripple, and more–in one great volume. Perfect inexpensive puzzler for clever youngsters. Full solutions. 112pp. 8⅛ x 11.
22951-3 Pa. $4.95

PIANO TUNING, J. Cree Fischer. Clearest, best book for beginner, amateur. Simple repairs, raising dropped notes, tuning by easy method of flattened fifths. No previous skills needed. 4 illustrations. 201pp. 5⅜ x 8½.   23267-0 Pa. $6.95

A SOURCE BOOK IN THEATRICAL HISTORY, A. M. Nagler. Contemporary observers on acting, directing, make-up, costuming, stage props, machinery, scene design, from Ancient Greece to Chekhov. 611pp. 5⅜ x 8½.   20515-0 Pa. $12.95

THE COMPLETE NONSENSE OF EDWARD LEAR, Edward Lear. All nonsense limericks, zany alphabets, Owl and Pussycat, songs, nonsense botany, etc., illustrated by Lear. Total of 320pp. 5⅜ x 8½. (USO)   20167-8 Pa. $6.95

VICTORIAN PARLOUR POETRY: An Annotated Anthology, Michael R. Turner. 117 gems by Longfellow, Tennyson, Browning, many lesser-known poets. "The Village Blacksmith," "Curfew Must Not Ring Tonight," "Only a Baby Small," dozens more, often difficult to find elsewhere. Index of poets, titles, first lines. xxiii + 325pp. 5⅜ x 8¼.   27044-0 Pa. $8.95

DUBLINERS, James Joyce. Fifteen stories offer vivid, tightly focused observations of the lives of Dublin's poorer classes. At least one, "The Dead," is considered a masterpiece. Reprinted complete and unabridged from standard edition. 160pp. 5³⁄₁₆ x 8¼.   26870-5 Pa. $1.00

THE HAUNTED MONASTERY and THE CHINESE MAZE MURDERS, Robert van Gulik. Two full novels by van Gulik, set in 7th-century China, continue adventures of Judge Dee and his companions. An evil Taoist monastery, seemingly supernatural events; overgrown topiary maze hides strange crimes. 27 illustrations. 328pp. 5⅜ x 8½.   23502-5 Pa. $8.95

THE BOOK OF THE SACRED MAGIC OF ABRAMELIN THE MAGE, translated by S. MacGregor Mathers. Medieval manuscript of ceremonial magic. Basic document in Aleister Crowley, Golden Dawn groups. 268pp. 5⅜ x 8½.   23211-5 Pa. $8.95

NEW RUSSIAN-ENGLISH AND ENGLISH-RUSSIAN DICTIONARY, M. A. O'Brien. This is a remarkably handy Russian dictionary, containing a surprising amount of information, including over 70,000 entries. 366pp. 4½ x 6⅛.   20208-9 Pa. $9.95

HISTORIC HOMES OF THE AMERICAN PRESIDENTS, Second, Revised Edition, Irvin Haas. A traveler's guide to American Presidential homes, most open to the public, depicting and describing homes occupied by every American President from George Washington to George Bush. With visiting hours, admission charges, travel routes. 175 photographs. Index. 160pp. 8¼ x 11.   26751-2 Pa. $11.95

NEW YORK IN THE FORTIES, Andreas Feininger. 162 brilliant photographs by the well-known photographer, formerly with *Life* magazine. Commuters, shoppers, Times Square at night, much else from city at its peak. Captions by John von Hartz. 181pp. 9¼ x 10¾.   23585-8 Pa. $12.95

INDIAN SIGN LANGUAGE, William Tomkins. Over 525 signs developed by Sioux and other tribes. Written instructions and diagrams. Also 290 pictographs. 111pp. 6⅛ x 9¼.   22029-X Pa. $3.95

ANATOMY: A Complete Guide for Artists, Joseph Sheppard. A master of figure drawing shows artists how to render human anatomy convincingly. Over 460 illustrations. 224pp. 8⅜ x 11¼. 27279-6 Pa. $10.95

MEDIEVAL CALLIGRAPHY: Its History and Technique, Marc Drogin. Spirited history, comprehensive instruction manual covers 13 styles (ca. 4th century thru 15th). Excellent photographs; directions for duplicating medieval techniques with modern tools. 224pp. 8⅜ x 11¼. 26142-5 Pa. $12.95

DRIED FLOWERS: How to Prepare Them, Sarah Whitlock and Martha Rankin. Complete instructions on how to use silica gel, meal and borax, perlite aggregate, sand and borax, glycerine and water to create attractive permanent flower arrangements. 12 illustrations. 32pp. 5⅜ x 8½. 21802-3 Pa. $1.00

EASY-TO-MAKE BIRD FEEDERS FOR WOODWORKERS, Scott D. Campbell. Detailed, simple-to-use guide for designing, constructing, caring for and using feeders. Text, illustrations for 12 classic and contemporary designs. 96pp. 5⅜ x 8½. 25847-5 Pa. $2.95

SCOTTISH WONDER TALES FROM MYTH AND LEGEND, Donald A. Mackenzie. 16 lively tales tell of giants rumbling down mountainsides, of a magic wand that turns stone pillars into warriors, of gods and goddesses, evil hags, powerful forces and more. 240pp. 5⅜ x 8½. 29677-6 Pa. $6.95

THE HISTORY OF UNDERCLOTHES, C. Willett Cunnington and Phyllis Cunnington. Fascinating, well-documented survey covering six centuries of English undergarments, enhanced with over 100 illustrations: 12th-century laced-up bodice, footed long drawers (1795), 19th-century bustles, 19th-century corsets for men, Victorian "bust improvers," much more. 272pp. 5⅜ x 8¼. 27124-2 Pa. $9.95

ARTS AND CRAFTS FURNITURE: The Complete Brooks Catalog of 1912, Brooks Manufacturing Co. Photos and detailed descriptions of more than 150 now very collectible furniture designs from the Arts and Crafts movement depict davenports, settees, buffets, desks, tables, chairs, bedsteads, dressers and more, all built of solid, quarter-sawed oak. Invaluable for students and enthusiasts of antiques, Americana and the decorative arts. 80pp. 6½ x 9¼. 27471-3 Pa. $8.95

HOW WE INVENTED THE AIRPLANE: An Illustrated History, Orville Wright. Fascinating firsthand account covers early experiments, construction of planes and motors, first flights, much more. Introduction and commentary by Fred C. Kelly. 76 photographs. 96pp. 8¼ x 11. 25662-6 Pa. $8.95

THE ARTS OF THE SAILOR: Knotting, Splicing and Ropework, Hervey Garrett Smith. Indispensable shipboard reference covers tools, basic knots and useful hitches; handsewing and canvas work, more. Over 100 illustrations. Delightful reading for sea lovers. 256pp. 5⅜ x 8½. 26440-8 Pa. $7.95

FRANK LLOYD WRIGHT'S FALLINGWATER: The House and Its History, Second, Revised Edition, Donald Hoffmann. A total revision—both in text and illustrations—of the standard document on Fallingwater, the boldest, most personal architectural statement of Wright's mature years, updated with valuable new material from the recently opened Frank Lloyd Wright Archives. "Fascinating"–*The New York Times*. 116 illustrations. 128pp. 9¼ x 10¾. 27430-6 Pa. $11.95

PHOTOGRAPHIC SKETCHBOOK OF THE CIVIL WAR, Alexander Gardner. 100 photos taken on field during the Civil War. Famous shots of Manassas Harper's Ferry, Lincoln, Richmond, slave pens, etc. 244pp. 10⅝ x 8¼.   22731-6 Pa. $9.95

FIVE ACRES AND INDEPENDENCE, Maurice G. Kains. Great back-to-the-land classic explains basics of self-sufficient farming. The one book to get. 95 illustrations. 397pp. 5⅜ x 8½.   20974-1 Pa. $7.95

SONGS OF EASTERN BIRDS, Dr. Donald J. Borror. Songs and calls of 60 species most common to eastern U.S.: warblers, woodpeckers, flycatchers, thrushes, larks, many more in high-quality recording.   Cassette and manual 99912-2 $9.95

A MODERN HERBAL, Margaret Grieve. Much the fullest, most exact, most useful compilation of herbal material. Gigantic alphabetical encyclopedia, from aconite to zedoary, gives botanical information, medical properties, folklore, economic uses, much else. Indispensable to serious reader. 161 illustrations. 888pp. 6½ x 9¼. 2-vol. set. (USO)   Vol. I: 22798-7 Pa. $9.95
      Vol. II: 22799-5 Pa. $9.95

HIDDEN TREASURE MAZE BOOK, Dave Phillips. Solve 34 challenging mazes accompanied by heroic tales of adventure. Evil dragons, people-eating plants, bloodthirsty giants, many more dangerous adversaries lurk at every twist and turn. 34 mazes, stories, solutions. 48pp. 8¼ x 11.   24566-7 Pa. $2.95

LETTERS OF W. A. MOZART, Wolfgang A. Mozart. Remarkable letters show bawdy wit, humor, imagination, musical insights, contemporary musical world; includes some letters from Leopold Mozart. 276pp. 5⅜ x 8½.   22859-2 Pa. $7.95

BASIC PRINCIPLES OF CLASSICAL BALLET, Agrippina Vaganova. Great Russian theoretician, teacher explains methods for teaching classical ballet. 118 illustrations. 175pp. 5⅜ x 8½.   22036-2 Pa. $5.95

THE JUMPING FROG, Mark Twain. Revenge edition. The original story of The Celebrated Jumping Frog of Calaveras County, a hapless French translation, and Twain's hilarious "retranslation" from the French. 12 illustrations. 66pp. 5⅜ x 8½.   22686-7 Pa. $3.95

BEST REMEMBERED POEMS, Martin Gardner (ed.). The 126 poems in this superb collection of 19th- and 20th-century British and American verse range from Shelley's "To a Skylark" to the impassioned "Renascence" of Edna St. Vincent Millay and to Edward Lear's whimsical "The Owl and the Pussycat." 224pp. 5⅜ x 8½.   27165-X Pa. $4.95

COMPLETE SONNETS, William Shakespeare. Over 150 exquisite poems deal with love, friendship, the tyranny of time, beauty's evanescence, death and other themes in language of remarkable power, precision and beauty. Glossary of archaic terms. 80pp. 5³⁄₁₆ x 8¼.   26686-9 Pa. $1.00

BODIES IN A BOOKSHOP, R. T. Campbell. Challenging mystery of blackmail and murder with ingenious plot and superbly drawn characters. In the best tradition of British suspense fiction. 192pp. 5⅜ x 8½.   24720-1 Pa. $6.95

THE WIT AND HUMOR OF OSCAR WILDE, Alvin Redman (ed.). More than 1,000 ripostes, paradoxes, wisecracks: Work is the curse of the drinking classes; I can resist everything except temptation; etc. 258pp. 5⅜ x 8½.   20602-5 Pa. $5.95

SHAKESPEARE LEXICON AND QUOTATION DICTIONARY, Alexander Schmidt. Full definitions, locations, shades of meaning in every word in plays and poems. More than 50,000 exact quotations. 1,485pp. 6½ x 9¼. 2-vol. set.
Vol. 1: 22726-X Pa. $16.95
Vol. 2: 22727-8 Pa. $16.95

SELECTED POEMS, Emily Dickinson. Over 100 best-known, best-loved poems by one of America's foremost poets, reprinted from authoritative early editions. No comparable edition at this price. Index of first lines. 64pp. 5³⁄₁₆ x 8¼.
26466-1 Pa. $1.00

CELEBRATED CASES OF JUDGE DEE (DEE GOONG AN), translated by Robert van Gulik. Authentic 18th-century Chinese detective novel; Dee and associates solve three interlocked cases. Led to van Gulik's own stories with same characters. Extensive introduction. 9 illustrations. 237pp. 5⅜ x 8½.   23337-5 Pa. $6.95

THE MALLEUS MALEFICARUM OF KRAMER AND SPRENGER, translated by Montague Summers. Full text of most important witchhunter's "bible," used by both Catholics and Protestants. 278pp. 6⅝ x 10.   22802-9 Pa. $12.95

SPANISH STORIES/CUENTOS ESPAÑOLES: A Dual-Language Book, Angel Flores (ed.). Unique format offers 13 great stories in Spanish by Cervantes, Borges, others. Faithful English translations on facing pages. 352pp. 5⅜ x 8½.
25399-6 Pa. $8.95

THE CHICAGO WORLD'S FAIR OF 1893: A Photographic Record, Stanley Appelbaum (ed.). 128 rare photos show 200 buildings, Beaux-Arts architecture, Midway, original Ferris Wheel, Edison's kinetoscope, more. Architectural emphasis; full text. 116pp. 8¼ x 11.   23990-X Pa. $9.95

OLD QUEENS, N.Y., IN EARLY PHOTOGRAPHS, Vincent F. Seyfried and William Asadorian. Over 160 rare photographs of Maspeth, Jamaica, Jackson Heights, and other areas. Vintage views of DeWitt Clinton mansion, 1939 World's Fair and more. Captions. 192pp. 8⅞ x 11.   26358-4 Pa. $12.95

CAPTURED BY THE INDIANS: 15 Firsthand Accounts, 1750-1870, Frederick Drimmer. Astounding true historical accounts of grisly torture, bloody conflicts, relentless pursuits, miraculous escapes and more, by people who lived to tell the tale. 384pp. 5⅜ x 8½.   24901-8 Pa. $8.95

THE WORLD'S GREAT SPEECHES, Lewis Copeland and Lawrence W. Lamm (eds.). Vast collection of 278 speeches of Greeks to 1970. Powerful and effective models; unique look at history. 842pp. 5⅜ x 8½.   20468-5 Pa. $14.95

THE BOOK OF THE SWORD, Sir Richard F. Burton. Great Victorian scholar/adventurer's eloquent, erudite history of the "queen of weapons"–from prehistory to early Roman Empire. Evolution and development of early swords, variations (sabre, broadsword, cutlass, scimitar, etc.), much more. 336pp. 6⅛ x 9¼.
25434-8 Pa. $9.95

AUTOBIOGRAPHY: The Story of My Experiments with Truth, Mohandas K. Gandhi. Boyhood, legal studies, purification, the growth of the Satyagraha (nonviolent protest) movement. Critical, inspiring work of the man responsible for the freedom of India. 480pp. 5⅜ x 8½. (USO) 24593-4 Pa. $8.95

CELTIC MYTHS AND LEGENDS, T. W. Rolleston. Masterful retelling of Irish and Welsh stories and tales. Cuchulain, King Arthur, Deirdre, the Grail, many more. First paperback edition. 58 full-page illustrations. 512pp. 5⅜ x 8½. 26507-2 Pa. $9.95

THE PRINCIPLES OF PSYCHOLOGY, William James. Famous long course complete, unabridged. Stream of thought, time perception, memory, experimental methods; great work decades ahead of its time. 94 figures. 1,391pp. 5⅜ x 8½. 2-vol. set.
Vol. I: 20381-6 Pa. $12.95
Vol. II: 20382-4 Pa. $12.95

THE WORLD AS WILL AND REPRESENTATION, Arthur Schopenhauer. Definitive English translation of Schopenhauer's life work, correcting more than 1,000 errors, omissions in earlier translations. Translated by E. F. J. Payne. Total of 1,269pp. 5⅜ x 8½. 2-vol. set. Vol. 1: 21761-2 Pa. $11.95
Vol. 2: 21762-0 Pa. $12.95

MAGIC AND MYSTERY IN TIBET, Madame Alexandra David-Neel. Experiences among lamas, magicians, sages, sorcerers, Bonpa wizards. A true psychic discovery. 32 illustrations. 321pp. 5⅜ x 8½. (USO) 22682-4 Pa. $8.95

THE EGYPTIAN BOOK OF THE DEAD, E. A. Wallis Budge. Complete reproduction of Ani's papyrus, finest ever found. Full hieroglyphic text, interlinear transliteration, word-for-word translation, smooth translation. 533pp. 6½ x 9¼.
21866-X Pa. $10.95

MATHEMATICS FOR THE NONMATHEMATICIAN, Morris Kline. Detailed, college-level treatment of mathematics in cultural and historical context, with numerous exercises. Recommended Reading Lists. Tables. Numerous figures. 641pp. 5⅜ x 8½.
24823-2 Pa. $11.95

THEORY OF WING SECTIONS: Including a Summary of Airfoil Data, Ira H. Abbott and A. E. von Doenhoff. Concise compilation of subsonic aerodynamic characteristics of NACA wing sections, plus description of theory. 350pp. of tables. 693pp. 5⅜ x 8½. 60586-8 Pa. $14.95

THE RIME OF THE ANCIENT MARINER, Gustave Doré, S. T. Coleridge. Doré's finest work; 34 plates capture moods, subtleties of poem. Flawless full-size reproductions printed on facing pages with authoritative text of poem. "Beautiful. Simply beautiful."–*Publisher's Weekly.* 77pp. 9¼ x 12. 22305-1 Pa. $6.95

NORTH AMERICAN INDIAN DESIGNS FOR ARTISTS AND CRAFTSPEOPLE, Eva Wilson. Over 360 authentic copyright-free designs adapted from Navajo blankets, Hopi pottery, Sioux buffalo hides, more. Geometrics, symbolic figures, plant and animal motifs, etc. 128pp. 8⅜ x 11. (EUK) 25341-4 Pa. $8.95

SCULPTURE: Principles and Practice, Louis Slobodkin. Step-by-step approach to clay, plaster, metals, stone; classical and modern. 253 drawings, photos. 255pp. 8⅛ x 11.
22960-2 Pa. $11.95

THE INFLUENCE OF SEA POWER UPON HISTORY, 1660–1783, A. T. Mahan. Influential classic of naval history and tactics still used as text in war colleges. First paperback edition. 4 maps. 24 battle plans. 640pp. 5⅜ x 8½. 25509-3 Pa. $12.95

THE STORY OF THE TITANIC AS TOLD BY ITS SURVIVORS, Jack Winocour (ed.). What it was really like. Panic, despair, shocking inefficiency, and a little heroism. More thrilling than any fictional account. 26 illustrations. 320pp. 5⅜ x 8½. 20610-6 Pa. $8.95

FAIRY AND FOLK TALES OF THE IRISH PEASANTRY, William Butler Yeats (ed.). Treasury of 64 tales from the twilight world of Celtic myth and legend: "The Soul Cages," "The Kildare Pooka," "King O'Toole and his Goose," many more. Introduction and Notes by W. B. Yeats. 352pp. 5⅜ x 8½. 26941-8 Pa. $8.95

BUDDHIST MAHAYANA TEXTS, E. B. Cowell and Others (eds.). Superb, accurate translations of basic documents in Mahayana Buddhism, highly important in history of religions. The Buddha-karita of Asvaghosha, Larger Sukhavativyuha, more. 448pp. 5⅜ x 8½. 25552-2 Pa. $12.95

ONE TWO THREE . . . INFINITY: Facts and Speculations of Science, George Gamow. Great physicist's fascinating, readable overview of contemporary science: number theory, relativity, fourth dimension, entropy, genes, atomic structure, much more. 128 illustrations. Index. 352pp. 5⅜ x 8½. 25664-2 Pa. $8.95

ENGINEERING IN HISTORY, Richard Shelton Kirby, et al. Broad, nontechnical survey of history's major technological advances: birth of Greek science, industrial revolution, electricity and applied science, 20th-century automation, much more. 181 illustrations. ". . . excellent . . ."–*Isis.* Bibliography. vii + 530pp. 5⅝ x 8¼. 26412-2 Pa. $14.95

DALÍ ON MODERN ART: The Cuckolds of Antiquated Modern Art, Salvador Dalí. Influential painter skewers modern art and its practitioners. Outrageous evaluations of Picasso, Cézanne, Turner, more. 15 renderings of paintings discussed. 44 calligraphic decorations by Dalí. 96pp. 5⅜ x 8½. (USO) 29220-7 Pa. $4.95

ANTIQUE PLAYING CARDS: A Pictorial History, Henry René D'Allemagne. Over 900 elaborate, decorative images from rare playing cards (14th–20th centuries): Bacchus, death, dancing dogs, hunting scenes, royal coats of arms, players cheating, much more. 96pp. 9¼ x 12¼. 29265-7 Pa. $11.95

MAKING FURNITURE MASTERPIECES: 30 Projects with Measured Drawings, Franklin H. Gottshall. Step-by-step instructions, illustrations for constructing handsome, useful pieces, among them a Sheraton desk, Chippendale chair, Spanish desk, Queen Anne table and a William and Mary dressing mirror. 224pp. 8⅛ x 11¼. 29338-6 Pa. $13.95

THE FOSSIL BOOK: A Record of Prehistoric Life, Patricia V. Rich et al. Profusely illustrated definitive guide covers everything from single-celled organisms and dinosaurs to birds and mammals and the interplay between climate and man. Over 1,500 illustrations. 760pp. 7½ x 10⅛. 29371-8 Pa. $29.95

Prices subject to change without notice.

Available at your book dealer or write for free catalog to Dept. GI, Dover Publications, Inc., 31 East 2nd St., Mineola, N.Y. 11501. Dover publishes more than 500 books each year on science, elementary and advanced mathematics, biology, music, art, literary history, social sciences and other areas.